Inspire and Motivate Through Performance Reviews:

A Step-by-Step Guide

Edited by National Press Publications

NATIONAL PRESS PUBLICATIONS

A Division of Rockhurst University Continuing Education Center, Inc.
6901 West 63rd Street • P.O. Box 2949 • Shawnee Mission, Kansas 66201-1349
1-800-258-7248 • 1-913-432-7757

Inspire and Motivate Through Performance Reviews: A Step-by-Step Guide

Published by National Press Publications, Inc.
Copyright 2000 National Press Publications, Inc.
A Division of Rockhurst University Continuing Education Center, Inc.

Printed in the United States of America

1 2 3 4 5 6 7 8 9 10

ISBN 1-55852-277-8

Table of Contents

1 HOW TO CREATE "SAME-SIDE-OF-THE-DESK" THINKING

The environment in which performance appraisals and reviews occur has a tremendous impact on their effectiveness in motivating employees to produce the desired behaviors. In this chapter, we will review the basics of how to create a positive, "win-win" environment for your employees.

Appraisals involve setting goals, judging the results achieved, and creating performance criteria that can be met and measured over and over again for each of your employees' job descriptions. You should focus on three things:

- Performance, not personalities

- Valid, concrete, relevant issues rather than subjective emotions and feelings

- Reaching agreement on what the employee is going to improve in his performance and what you are going to do

In conducting performance appraisals, you need to make it very clear that *your objective is performance, not personality issues.* This is a big step toward "same-side-of-the-desk" thinking. Together, you and your employee both look at what can be done to solve performance problems.

How Not to Do It

Supervisor: You are always late. Some people in your department think you are lazy.

Employee: I am not lazy. If you think that, you don't understand me at all.

By implying that the employee is lazy, personality issues, emotions and defenses immediately take over. Saying that the employee is always late isn't quantified. Instead, to make it a factual performance issue, it must be measurable for five days out of the last 15, for example.

How to Do It

Supervisor: You have been late 10 of the last 30 days. You're missing key account calls.

Employee: I didn't realize it was that much! I'm always behind with my key accounts. That's probably why.

Supervisor: Is there anything I can do to help you?

By focusing on specific, often numeric or recorded information, the facts become the facts, rather than feelings. Facts can be addressed. Feelings escalate and become the foundation for self-justification, blame and continued poor performance.

How Not to Do It

Supervisor: You are always late. You are never here when your key accounts call.

Employee: I haven't been late that much … *(Thinking … you just don't like me, so you are exaggerating)* Get off my back.

How to Do It

Supervisor: You need to focus on being here on time. Some of your customers call you at 8:00 a.m., and you're not here to take care of them.

Employee: You are right. I can't get the same level of sales from them as from my other customers. Maybe that's the reason.

Supervisor: Is there anything I can do to help you?

Performance Appraisal Essentials

Be very clear in your communications. Use a 1-2-3 format:

1. Attempt to eliminate any misunderstandings.

2. Quantify specifically what is expected from the employee.

3. Describe exactly when it is expected.

The attitude you want to take is that you and the employee are partners in successful problem-solving.

How Not to Do It

Supervisor: This can't continue. If you don't change, there will be serious consequences.

Employee: OK. I'll do better.

In this episode, you use threats but no measurement; you have expectations with no consequences and specify no time frame when action will be taken.

How to Do It

Supervisor: This can't continue. Beginning tomorrow you are expected to be here by 8:00 a.m. to handle your job. If you are not here, I will give key accounts that call in to another representative. When your key accounts decline by 10 percent, your salary will be adjusted accordingly, and if they decline by 20 percent, we will reassign your area to someone else.

Employee: That's pretty harsh. I'm just a little late.

Supervisor: No. You are missing key contact calls because you are a "little" late, as you call it.

These are the basic components of good performance communications. If you are successful in executing the basic components, you gain the following advantages:

- You are forced to assess and realize that an employee's poor performance could be the result of inadequate management. Your attention is focused on what you need to do and say. Once you realize the role you play, the steps you take can focus the relationship between you and your employee, helping it to function productively on an adult-to-adult level.

- You provide employees with feedback on their performance, enabling them to learn what's expected to become a more successful member of your team.

- You can recognize and reinforce good performance and set goals for the future. When goals are set by the employee, there is more motivation to achieve those goals.

- You are given another tool for helping employees solve problems, one of your most important tools ... the tool that gets results!

The performance appraisal process provides useful feedback, helping you and your company optimize human assets. New goals and objectives are agreed upon, and work teams can be restructured for maximum efficiency. The development of your department must reflect the interests, abilities and motivations of the employees who comprise it; otherwise, achieving objectives will be nearly impossible. These goals emerge through the "same-side-of-the-desk" thinking of a well-planned performance system.

The ongoing feedback serves as the basis for you and your employee to strengthen your relationship and become a solid team, two adults working toward a common, agreed-upon goal. It forces you to look at your own actions to see what supervision the employee requires for better performance. Your job is to quickly identify the techniques that work with individual employees and adjust your own style to get the maximum productivity from each of your employees.

Leadership, Your Style and Performance Improvement

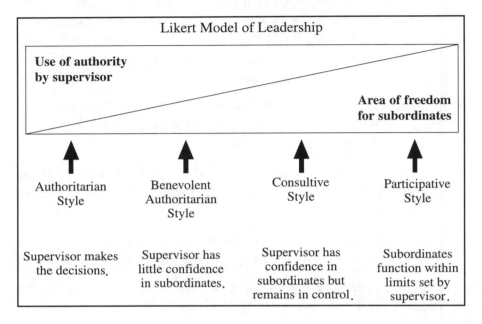

Likert Model of Leadership

Look at each end of this chart, beginning on the left side. Some employees cannot deal with too much independent decision making. They need a supervisor to decide and direct their work, using an authoritarian style.

Authoritarian

Employee: I don't know how to handle the call to ABC Company. They never respond, and I never get a sale with them. I just don't know what to do.

Supervisor: Handle them as we handled that call with XYZ Company. You offered to go over to see their operation. They liked that, and that opened the door for you. Call them right now.

Employee: You are right. That's what I need to do!

Participative

Supervisor: What problem might you encounter in handling the DEF Company account?

Employee: I can't get them to make a commitment. We're just one of a number of companies calling on them right now. They think our product is a commodity, and they want to buy only on price.

Supervisor: How do you think you should handle it?

Employee: I would like to invite them over for a tour of our facility to show them how advanced we are in quality management. I think we can distinguish ourselves from the competition in that area and show them the value added with our products … that there really is a difference, not only with our products but also with our people.

Supervisor: That's a fine idea. How can I help?

You'll notice that in the last example the supervisor lets the employee solve his own problem (participative). In contrast, in the first example (authoritarian), direct commands are given for the employee to execute. The supervisor knows that the employee will execute them well but will have trouble seeing the right thing to do on his own, so the supervisor tells the employee in no uncertain terms (authoritarian) what should be done.

Your leadership style must change with different issues and different employees. This is not the same as being wishy-washy or a constantly changing person whom no one can get a fix on. It means that you carefully consider what will work for each individual and situationally apply a technique or a series of techniques to accomplish the objective. This does not mean bearing the entire responsibility for your subordinate's performance yourself. The employee has equal responsibility. But it's your job, as a leader, to see that he has been provided with everything necessary to meet his job responsibilities.

When employees hear performance feedback from a well-done appraisal session, they have real, solid information to act on. Without such information, they're guessing, and their record usually indicates inadequacies. Time spent guessing is wasted, unproductive time. You can't afford to have your people work in a "guessing" mode, and neither can your company.

How Not to Do It

Supervisor: So, let's close by focusing on the fact that you need to make more good sales calls each day.

Employee: *(After the meeting)* My supervisor talked about how I needed to make more good calls each day. But what's a "good" call? I guess I'll just make more calls. Obviously, the company is only interested in the number of calls, not how well they're done or the results. I'll just fill up my call sheet ...

You can see in the above example that the supervisor's guidance is incomplete. What really constitutes a "good" sales call? The employee may increase the number of calls, but is left guessing how to improve the quality or the results.

How to Do It

Supervisor: So let's close by focusing on the fact that you need to make XX number of good sales calls each day.

Employee: OK.

Supervisor: Just to be sure we're on the same wavelength, let's review the components of a good sales call. Each call should ... *(detail expectations)*. Are you comfortable with each of those areas, or is there something else I can do to help?

Employee: I understand now what is expected.

Positive Performance Feedback

Sometimes when people think of performance reviews, they think only of the negative. While it is important to put out the most threatening fires, giving positive feedback to employees is very important. This is especially true when employees have just made a difficult change. They need to know you're watching and recognizing their work and that they're achieving results.

If you do have negative feedback to give, a well-known successful technique, called "insertion," usually proves successful. First a positive comment is made, then the negative feedback is "inserted" and a positive comment finally closes. The overall effect on the employee is positive while a negative concern still is being addressed. This technique is especially useful with an employee who is trying, making progress or doesn't handle criticism well. It's not recommended where stern warnings are required, however.

How to Do It

Supervisor: I really like the way you've taken control of the DEF account. *(Positive)*

Employee: Thank you. It felt good to finally get them as a regular customer.

Supervisor: The TUV account is causing a lot of problems. *(Negative)* We need to discuss what to do about it. You handled the ABC account well. *(Positive)* How can we use what we learned on ABC to solve the problems with TUV?

The performance appraisal process helps determine where an employee is in his development and helps the company better deploy the skill sets of its employees to achieve the business objectives. Here are a few tips you'll find helpful:

Remember: Real-time feedback motivates!

- The time to correct an employee's mistake is when it happens. Don't allow an error to become a habit.

- The performance appraisal process should be a summary of the day-to-day realizations the employee and you share.

- The magic isn't in the appraisal form … it's in the people trying to work together to create a better future.

- Properly conducted, the performance appraisal process provides as much relationship improvement as performance improvement.

- There should never be surprises at the formal, year-end performance review. If there are, many opportunities for improvement and strengthening throughout the year have been lost.

The pace of business today is hectic and will likely continue as the trend toward downsizing/rightsizing continues and worldwide competitive pressures increase. The time to talk about good or bad performance is when it happens, when the issues are clear and not influenced by the rush of memories.

Employees become motivated when they feel you are there with them, caring, coaching and understanding the events that occur. You want to stop something before it becomes larger, so by dealing with it quickly, you can get it out of the way and move on to other matters, like increasing productivity. By dealing with things as they happen, you also avoid festering feelings.

Communication Basics

The major reasons for performance problems are lack of direction and lack of feedback … in other words, lack of effective communication. You are responsible for making sure your message is understood. You must learn to "say what you mean and mean what you say."

Our mind thinks at least six times faster than we can speak. Messages that are seen, heard and understood by doing are the most likely to be retained.

Ten Ways to Keep a
Performance-Correction Conversation Positive

1. Confront in private.

2. Assume the employee wants to do a good job.

3. Have a plan and don't deliver an ultimatum.

4. Use the positive, counseling approach.

5. Control your own emotions.

6. Criticize the behavior, not the person.

7. Be aware of positive terms to use and inflammatory words to avoid when confronting.

8. Avoid labeling; use nonjudgmental, factual statements.

9. Communicate why the behavior must be changed — and the benefit to the employee.

10. Brainstorm solutions together.

Because the mind receives information so quickly, it often reacts even before the message is completed. Instead of viewing communication as information transmission (as many do), consider it more as idea transmission. That is, say or do something that will cause that idea to appear in your employee's head and ask the employee to speak back, restating the idea so you have conclusive proof it's in there! In this way, you verify that he is involved. You have to think of a way to make the employee say it, for example, by asking questions. Therefore, you can improve communication with your employees by learning basic questioning skills.

An effective communicator learns to ask preparation questions. Before you ever talk to an employee, you must master the nine key preparation questions.

1. What background information exists?

2. What specific behaviors are at issue?

3. What are the consequences if things go unchanged?

4. What is the immediate objective?

5. What is my long-range goal?

6. What are the benefits of changed behavior?

7. How can this issue be described in the present tense?

8. How can I support this employee?

9. Am I in control and ready to discuss this situation?

It's also good to rehearse questions you can ask if an employee is shy, very quiet or resistant to your appraisal of him. Too often managers and supervisors find themselves talking too much during the appraisal and getting little or no employee feedback. Ask open-ended questions and then wait for a response. If you wait long enough, the employee will respond … he won't be able to stand the silence.

The Formal, Sit-Down Performance Appraisal

If you realize you have failed to change your employee's behavior through daily interaction, you can use the formal, sit-down performance appraisal to finally get your point across.

Properly handled, the formal, sit-down performance appraisal becomes a summary of observations as well as a solid platform for new understanding of how to achieve the best results possible.

Once you observe less than optimal results, it's time to revisit your employee's job description. It describes accepted expectations and offers a format for discussing where performance has slipped. The employee can then modify his actions, and you can provide appropriate help. An honest discussion of shortfalls and performance results should refocus both you and your employee. The format itself is only a guideline to help the conversation focus productively.

The magic comes when the two people communicate, break through their problems and obstacles, celebrate their success and plan for more. The employee in this framework feels a part of the process rather than a victim of it. The relationship between team members also can improve.

Performance improvement often follows naturally because you took time to refocus your employee's personal pride. Employees are normally highly motivated with a desire to please. Use this to your advantage in directing their actions and building your relationship with them.

Requirements for Effective Appraisals

Open Discussion: Research studies show employees are more satisfied with their appraisal results if they have the chance to talk freely about their performance.

Constructive Intention: Employees must recognize that negative feedback is provided with the intent to improve their future performance. If feedback is perceived as destructive criticism (vague, unfair, or harshly presented), problems such as anger, resentment and tension result … causing further deterioration of performance.

Set Performance Goals: Goals stimulate employee effort, focus attention, increase persistence and encourage employees to find new and better ways to do their work.

A Credible Appraiser: Appraisers must be well-informed. They should be respected by the employee. Appraisers should be comfortable with the appraisal process and knowledgeable about the employee's job and performance.

1. Do your employees have a clear understanding of exactly what is expected of them? What misunderstandings or points of clarification should you address immediately? Be specific.

2. Review your most recent "corrective conversations" with each of your employees.

   • Was your style authoritarian or participative?

   • Was each focused on performance rather than personality issues?

   • Did each address facts or were emotions and judgments allowed to become part of the equation?

   • Did you get agreement from each employee to a specific improvement plan?

3. Use the questions on page 12 to prepare yourself for your next conversation with each subordinate.

Reflections

2 LEGAL ISSUES

Your company's performance appraisal system is central to nearly all personnel processes: hiring, promotion, demotion, transfer, salary, selection for training, etc. This book will not focus on all the legal ramifications; you need to talk to your legal counsel about such matters. This chapter is designed to give you a brief overview.

Employment Law

Uniform Guidelines on Employee Selection 1978 is the controlling federal law in the area of performance appraisals.

Your performance appraisal must have **no adverse impact** on any of the areas covered by the law, such as employees':

- Race
- Sex
- Religion
- National origin
- Age
- Handicapped status

These are the major areas covered, but they may not describe all the areas protected by law when you read this. Consult your company's training guide or your personnel manager about any questions. Most well-run companies will train you in-depth in conducting performance appraisals and other related personnel issues as they hold much of the legal liability.

Your performance reviews must be workable, equitable, ongoing and as objective as possible, for you and your organization are expected to follow and meet all legal requirements. Lack of knowledge or ignorance of the law is no excuse for violations. You must understand that if a member of any "protected" group is adversely affected, the performance appraisal practice is illegal. All performance appraisal practices must contain measuring standards. What does this mean?

Special Tip: Questions about anti-discrimination laws and the current enforcement policies of the Equal Employment Opportunity Commission can be directed to agency experts through a nationwide free information hot line. Dial (800) USA-EEOC. Calls made from a touch-tone phone will be answered by a recording, but you can talk to a specialist by dialing "2" after you hear the recording.

Measuring Standards

Measuring standards are valid when you can:

1. Prove content validity — a person must be able to perform this task to do her job.

2. Prove construct validity — you must show the relationship between rating scores and traits or skills needed on the job.

3. Prove criterion-related validity — you must show the relationship between rating scores and measure of job performance.

In other words, in order to be legal, a certain skill must be shown to be a valid, true and necessary requirement of the job. Discrimination against protected groups is allowable as long as the discriminating variable is legitimately related to the requirements of the work situation. For example, if the next level job on the factory floor demands the ability to lift 75 pounds above waist height, and a wheelchair-bound employee cannot perform this task, it is acceptable not to promote that person to that job.

You must be able to consistently observe the employee performing the assigned tasks. Your rating criteria must be the same for all employees of the same grade/class/group. But be careful, because using numerical scores increases an organization's liability to validate them. Just because something is expressed in numbers does not automatically make it legal.

Another important aspect to consider is the employee's right to privacy. Employees must have complete access to their personnel files, but others should have controlled access. These records must be accurate, relevant and current. Discuss with your personnel department any questions you have in these areas, but keep in mind that job-relatedness and fairness are the two controlling principles whenever you put something in writing.

Substantial performance, or even average performance, should not be described in such a way that the employee believes her performance is better than it is. You do a great disservice to your employee and your team when you praise what's less than adequate performance. Besides, you flirt with performance collapse. Employees soon lose confidence in you, their trust sags and respect falls.

Performance Standards

Written standards should be the basis of performance appraisals so that:

- It is clear to both supervisor and employees what needs to be done.

- Everyone can identify whether it is being done.

- Everyone can tell whether it's being done in an acceptable way.

- Everyone can know when corrective action will take place.

Performance must be described *accurately* and must be based on *documentation*. If an employee is terminated for poor performance, but previous reviews were either good or vague, the employee may have grounds for a wrongful discharge lawsuit. All performance appraisal feedback as well as any other employee communication must be free of sexual innuendo or sexual harassment.

WARNING! Be careful of rating subjective qualities: attitude, cooperation, enthusiasm, initiative. Subjective ratings are difficult for you or your company to defend in court. Quantifiable areas such as deadlines met, calls made, items produced, quota achieved, etc., are much easier to defend and are more productive for you and your employee.

1. What is your current depth of understanding of employment law?

2. Identify the areas where your knowledge is most limited and detail a plan to improve your proficiency in each of those areas.

3. Take a close look at your current performance review process and its impact on promotions, transfers, raises, reprimands, etc. Try to look from the perspective of individuals in each of the protected categories.

   • Are there obvious areas of concern? Be specific.

   • How solid are your measuring standards? What areas could use some refining?

   • What can you do to strengthen your performance appraisal process?

Reflections

3 WHAT EMPLOYERS AND EMPLOYEES NEED FROM THE APPRAISAL PROCESS

Effective performance appraisal systems are designed to meet the needs of both employers and employees. This chapter will outline the most critical areas to be addressed to create a mutually satisfying system.

Employer Needs

The employee is an asset of the company, and the employer needs to regularly review and productively direct the contributions that employees make toward achieving the company's objectives. As a manager or supervisor, you must focus on the needs of your organization, including:

1. Performance appraisals that help control quality, performance and output

2. A system that identifies both individual employee and departmental training needs

3. Necessary information for manpower and organizational planning

4. Recommendations that reinforce or suggest modifications to the employee selection process

5. A performance system that improves employee morale and offers recognition and reward for above-average performance

6. An opportunity to talk about how to develop particular employees

7. Time to talk about the job and what needs to be done to improve

8. A chance to motivate, teach and coach. (This area is often not clearly recognized by either employer or employee.)

The respect, rights and responsibilities of the employee, the supervisor and the organization must be kept in balance.

Employee Needs

1. To know how/what he is doing relative to your expectations and the company's goals

2. To understand the following:

   • The criteria to be used in the performance appraisal

   • How his performance will be measured (against which standard)

   • Who will do the appraisal

   • When the appraisal will be done

   • What feedback he will get

   • If he can give input to the process and when

   • What assistance the company will provide in improving performance

   • What the rewards are for above-average performance

3. To be listened to in the following areas:

   • How things are going on the job in general

   • Any specific problems he is experiencing

- What you, as supervisor, can do to make his job less frustrating and him more effective

- What the employee thinks he is doing well and suggested areas for improvement

4. To receive helpful, constructive feedback

5. To be treated with dignity and respect

6. To feel that someone cares

There are several other factors to consider when looking at the relationship between employee performance appraisals and your employee's needs:

1. The employee's desire to be evaluated varies both within each individual and from individual to individual over time. An individual who believes his performance is good is less concerned about the opinions of others regarding performance. An individual who is success-oriented in his performance is more interested in feedback than one who fears failure.

2. The anticipation of being evaluated is threatening. Therefore, hostility is often directed toward performance appraisers. An employee often views an evaluation as an occasion when he lacks control of his fate, and he is frequently apprehensive and anxious. Individuals with low self-esteem are more apt to feel threatened than those with high self-esteem. Negative reactions to criticism often occur if ongoing support is not available from you.

3. The more an individual is able to influence his evaluator, the more likely he is to accept an evaluation as his own evaluation. The relationship between a supervisor and his associates determines whether the latter accept the former's ratings. An expert appraiser's opinions are more likely to be accepted than those of a nonexpert. Your staff is more likely to accept your ratings if they like and respect you, and an individual is more likely to accept evaluations that are similar to those he has received from other appraisers.

A mutuality develops when you pay attention to your employee's needs, and a true sense of respect emerges when your own and the organization's needs are shared with the employee.

Benefits of Appraisal

- Motivation and Satisfaction

- Training and Development

- Recruitment and Induction

- Employee Evaluation

---

1. Have you clearly detailed for each of your employees how his individual performance relates to the success of the organization as a whole? Can each see himself as part of the "Big Picture"?

2. Do all employees understand the exact criteria to be used in their performance appraisals? If they were asked today to write down the five most important aspects of their performance, could they do it ... and match your list?

3. Do your employees feel your feedback is helpful, or do they feel threatened by the performance review?

4. Rate yourself on a scale of 1 - 10 (10 being highest) on how much dignity and respect you afford your subordinates. Rate yourself on each individual and on the group as a whole. Then have your employees rate you on how much dignity and respect they feel. What changes do you need to make to bring those perspectives more in line with each other?

Reflections
Reflections

4 THE PERFORMANCE APPRAISAL SYSTEM

There are numerous types of appraisal systems — each with its own unique set of advantages and disadvantages in various situations and types of organizations. This chapter is devoted to enhancing your understanding of appraisal system choices. Carefully read the description of each type of system. You will find ideas you can use, no matter what style your company currently follows.

Types of Appraisal Systems

- Self-Directed Work Teams

- Peer Appraisal

- Self-Rating Systems Combined With Formal Performance Appraisal

- Rating Scales

- Free-Form Essay

- Results — MBO

- Forced-Rank Comparisons

Self-Directed Work Teams

Overview: In this model, the performance appraisal is the primary vehicle for communicating business strategy to employees. Each team has a family of critical measures linked to measures of performance that, in turn, constitute the overall business strategy. These measures are revised annually.

Description: Performance measures usually fall into the following groups:

- Quality

- Financial — cost and revenue considerations

- Timeliness

- Productivity/efficiency

Associated with each measure are three criteria: a long-term goal, short-term goals and the minimum standards of performance.

Teams usually:

- Identify behaviors that have the greatest impact on performance.

- Measure behavior and create specific feedback on team performance compared to the goal. Employees keep track of their own performance. Weekly and monthly team meetings are held to identify problems and work through solutions.

- Rely on managers who are trained to reinforce desired behavior as it occurs, not just once or twice a year.

Individual employee performance goals center primarily on learning and development. Goals for an individual might be to improve communication or build problem-solving skills. General actions to achieve these goals might be taking on more leadership responsibilities in meetings (communication) or serving on a task force (problem-solving). Specific tactics might include working on different communication or problem-solving techniques.

Personal contribution to the team's goals might include: quality improvement, cost reduction or improvements in customer service. Team goals clarify the role of the work group. Work groups are charged with the responsibility to accomplish a "family of measures," five to 10 key measures of performance that the team must monitor, control and improve.

In summary, the self-directed work team performance appraisal system is one type of system used by companies that utilize work teams. This system allows you to conduct short, ongoing, informal reviews as well as formal reviews every quarter. It provides the freedom to structure the review in light of individual and team needs. It is not just a paperwork exercise but real, ongoing communication with no once-a-year surprises.

Peer Appraisal

Overview: Sometimes you may use this technique to gain additional information, especially when using work teams.

Description: The employee is reviewed by her peers. Feedback is collected from team members, compiled by the appraiser and used in combination with a more traditional appraisal form.

Advantages: A well-rounded view of performance can be gained by combining a variety of perspectives. It also builds peer accountability.

Disadvantages: You may need to build the veracity and commitment of your employees. Helping them feel good about the process takes time. Here are some guidelines to making a peer evaluation system work:

1. Start small. Don't try to get everyone to appraise everyone. Begin with one or two peer evaluations. Sometimes the employee picks her own peer evaluators.

2. Protect the confidentiality of all peer ratings. Truthfulness and honest feedback increase when peers know their specific insights will not be exposed. Your employee needs to know how she is perceived by the team, not necessarily the specifics.

3. When peers know that performance and income potential come from these ratings, it is very tempting to write favorable reviews. No one wants to take food from someone else. It's important that you de-emphasize punishment, emphasize positive criticism and keep everyone focused on team success.

4. Do not abdicate your managerial responsibilities to the peer review. The peer review offers valuable information that should support and affirm the key points you choose to appraise. If you are out of step with an employee's peer reviews, rethink your perceptions.

Self-Rating Systems Combined With Formal Performance Appraisal

Overview: Self-rating creates a participative approach to the traditional appraisal method. Employees rate their performance and then review it with you. This is the method we will expand upon in an upcoming section, "The Employee Self-Analysis." You can change the rating to reflect the true situation if the employee has rated herself too high or too low. Responsibility for the performance appraisal is delegated to the employee. This method treats people like adults. Your role truly becomes one of counselor, teacher and coach.

Description: Ninety percent of all self-appraisals rate employees at or below what you would! This high percentage makes the method viable. Your role becomes one of praising, encouraging and being generally positive to the employee. The employee comes away with a better self-image.

If an employee rates herself correctly, your role becomes one of confirmation and reinforcement. This leads naturally into a "Where do we go from here?" attitude, opening up exploration of further development and improvement.

Ten percent of employees will rate themselves higher than the manager does. Half of them genuinely believe their performance is that good, and this calls for a response from you. These employees usually aren't trying to fight about their rating; they simply have a different perception. The other half, however, are the employees who are not happy under any performance appraisal system. They have inflated opinions of themselves, and they argue with whatever weaknesses the manager addresses.

Advantages: Self-rating stands up well in court defenses. Fewer cases go to court when the employee participates in her own performance appraisal than when appraisals are completed only by supervisors.

Rating Scales

Overview: Behaviorally anchored rating scales are charted. Key issues are targeted and measured. You sample behavior over the long term and do not rely on short-range judgments and impressions. Such scales reveal the complex behaviors that contribute to successful performance.

Description: The rating scales method offers a high degree of structure for appraisals. Each employee trait or characteristic is rated on a bipolar scale that usually has several points ranging from "poor" to "excellent."

Rating scale appraisals are popular because organizations can use a common "one-size-fits-all" form that can be administered quickly and easily. They also give the appearance of objectivity and perception of fairness — false though they may be.

Advantages: The greatest advantage of rating scales is that they are structured and standardized — allowing ratings to be compared and contrasted across an entire organization. Each employee is subjected to the same basic process and rating criteria.

Rating scale methods are easy to use and understand. The concept of the rating scale makes sense; both managers and subordinates have an appreciation for the simple logic of the bipolar scale.

Disadvantages: The disadvantages of rating scales are many:

1. Trait relevance: It is inevitable that with a standardized appraisal system, some traits will have a greater relevance to some jobs than to others. For example, "initiative" may be unimportant in a tightly structured position, so a low rating on "initiative" might reflect that the employee had few opportunities to display initiative — rather than a lack of skill or drive in that area.

2. Fairness/perceptual problems: Problems of perceived meaning occur when appraisers do not share the same opinion about the meaning of the selected traits and the language used on the rating scale. For example, one appraiser might view an employee's reporting problems to a supervisor as displaying initiative — while another might perceive it as an excessive dependence on supervisory assistance. Even the terminology "performance exceeds expectations" or "below average skill" may mean different things to different appraisers.

   In addition, one must watch for the halo or horns effect as well. Selective perception is the human tendency to make highly subjective assessments of a person's capability — then seek evidence to support that view while ignoring evidence to the contrary.

3. Appearance of objectivity: Rating systems give people a false sense of security, protection and objectivity. Because of our desire to be objective, we create systems that use numerical scales (e.g., 1 - 5) to rate employees — and base pay and promotion decisions on that numerical information — often ignoring that the numerical score is based on subjective information. We forget that any rating is an indication of how ONE person applies a fuzzy criterion.

4. Development issues: Rating systems alone do not convey sufficient information for people to improve. Much more detail and documentation are needed regarding exactly what the individual must do and what changes are to be made.

Free-Form Essay

Overview: This system usually consists of a description, in the appraiser's words, of the employee's overall performance, including quantity and quality of work, job know-how, and ability to get along with other employees. The appraiser lists both the employee's good points and shortcomings as well as suggestions for courses of action to remedy problem areas. This statement may be prepared by the appraiser alone or be done in collaboration with the appraisee.

Advantages: The free-form essay method allows appraisers to examine almost any relevant issue or attribute of performance. They are free from rigidly defined appraisal criteria and may place whatever degree of emphasis on issues or attributes they feel appropriate. Thus the process is open-ended and very flexible.

Disadvantages: Essay methods are time-consuming and difficult to administer. The varying writing skills of appraisers can further distort an already subjective process. It is difficult to compare results of individuals and to draw valid conclusions across an organization.

Results — MBO

Overview: MBO (Management By Objectives) methods of appraisal are results-oriented. They seek to measure employee performance by examining the extent to which predetermined objectives have been achieved.

Description: The use of management objectives was first advocated in the 1950s by Peter Drucker. The objectives are established jointly by the supervisor and subordinate. The employee is typically expected to identify the skills and tools needed to achieve results and is expected to monitor her own development and progress.

Advantages: MBO methods can give employees a satisfying sense of autonomy and achievement. Employees are judged according to real outcomes — not their potential for success or someone's subjective opinion of their abilities.

33

Disadvantages: MBO methods can lead to unrealistic expectations about what can and cannot be accomplished. Both managers and employees must have excellent "reality-checking" skills in order to be able to set realistic objectives and to self-audit and self-monitor. Research indicates that most people lack the skills necessary to be their own "reality checker."

A further disadvantage is the inherent rigidity of objectives. In an era of constant change, flexibility is required of any organization that wants to survive. More flexible objectives may lead to less clarity and more subjectivity in the appraisal process.

Forced-Rank Comparisons

Overview: These are based on the selection of one statement that the appraiser thinks most accurately describes employee behavior from three to five alternatives. Each statement is weighted; therefore, employees with higher scores are deemed to be better than employees with lower scores.

Description: The core element of rankings is that employees are compared to one another and given a number that (supposedly) indicates whether they are better than, about the same or less effective than their colleagues. The criteria for ranking can range from specific and objective to fuzzy and subjective. The ranking is then often used to determine raises and promotions.

Advantages: In some environments, the competitive nature of the ranking system can encourage staff to push each other to greater productivity. Organizations that rely on merit assessments for pay and promotion decisions use the forced rank to determine the "top 10 percent" that will be eligible for consideration.

Disadvantages: Ranking systems don't assess value and contribution, even in a best-case scenario. The value of an employee relative to peers is irrelevant to the success of an organization. What really matters is their absolute contribution to the success of the organization.

Ranking is virtually useless as a form of feedback. To develop our people, we need to provide specific, concrete feedback — not some nebulous ranking within a unit of undefined quality.

Ranking can be devastating to the morale of an organization. Ranking guarantees disagreement.

List two characteristics of each type of appraisal system. Then identify how you can use that information to make your own performance appraisals more effective.

Appraisal System Type	Characteristics	How to Use This Information
Self-Directed Work Teams	1.	
	2.	
Peer Appraisal	1.	
	2.	
Self-Rating Systems Combined With Formal Review	1.	
	2.	
Rating Scales	1.	
	2.	
Free-Form Essay	1.	
	2.	
Results — MBO	1.	
	2.	
Forced Rank Comparisons	1.	
	2.	

Reflections

5 THE PERFORMANCE INTERVIEW

The actual performance interview is not the beginning or the end of anything. It is the middle step in a continuing, repetitive cycle, with the content of each discussion changing. In this chapter, we'll explore various aspects of the performance interview.

An Overview

Your first step is to define the job. Don't be content with a job description that is supplied to you. Look at it carefully to see if it truly relates to your department, your company and your goals TODAY! Ask yourself, "What is it I really want my employee to do?" And if there's more than a 10 percent change from what's written in the job description, rewrite it! Better yet, write it with your employee.

Your second step is to communicate the job effectively to the employee, leveling on what is expected. This goes beyond handing your employee written job specs. It goes to the heart of what is expected and, if appropriate, the when and the how.

The third step in the appraisal cycle is keeping a performance log on each employee and updating it frequently. The performance log contains the date, the event, the action taken, the result and the follow-up information on each employee. These are primarily incident reports, including progress reports where you evaluate work in progress. Pick a time period each week to update these logs. It is necessary not only to document extraordinary events but also to make summary entries. Stick to the facts in your entries. Personal feelings or opinions will not be helpful to you later.

The actual performance appraisal should not be too extensive; after all, everyone fails periodically. The purpose of the appraisal is not to communicate all your judgments. You must learn to limit yourself, covering what's possible. You control the appraisal. What you want to accomplish determines how you plan and conduct an appraisal.

- Set your objectives.

- Determine what will be talked about.

- Keep the interview on track.

By keeping the interview on track, you get the employee to want to improve his performance. The key to successful appraisals is being able to answer "yes" to each of these questions:

- Does the employee know what is expected?

- Have you developed objectives for the interview based on your desired results?

- Will you control the appraisal interview and not let an appraisal form do it?

- Have you developed a strategy for the appraisal interview?

- Do you have the necessary skills to do what you want to do?

If you cannot answer "yes" to each of these questions, you are not ready to discuss performance with your employee.

The Appraisal Form

Before you can become proficient in each aspect of conducting a successful performance appraisal, you must understand how your company expects the performance appraisal to be used. After understanding your company's policy, consider the following topics:

1. Make sure the form serves your needs as well as the needs of the employee you will be rating. Normally, forms cover too much. If the form is too overwhelming, it's not helpful. Further, when a form deals with attitudes and other abstract behavior, how do you get objective measurements? Abstract behavior is not as objective an assessment as "five days late in the last 30-day period," yet it is often treated as such. How will you keep from having a negative impact on performance when using the form?

2. The performance appraisal form is not your only basis for employee appraisal. Don't fill out the form and send it in without consulting the employee, but don't change the form after discussing it with the employee.

3. Everyone should view and use appraisals professionally. Appraisals are personal and privileged information.

4. Appraisal forms should call for objective data on the employee's performance. Performance should be rated as "satisfactory" or "unsatisfactory" with a space for comments. You and the employee should work on the form together. Each of you should review a blank form in preparation for the meeting and then complete the form in the meeting, utilizing joint discussion without preconceptions.

This approach usually results in the most successful appraisals. You are free to conduct a purposeful appraisal interview without the constrictions of the form. If a form is required, use it. But don't let the form limit a meaningful performance discussion with your employee.

Preparing for the Performance Appraisal

The following points offer you a step-by-step method for analyzing employee behavior. By looking carefully at your employee's performance and writing down specifics to discuss, you will feel prepared. This helps build your own confidence and results in a more positive experience for both you and the employee.

The basis for this preparation is a review of your performance log. Review each incident report and progress report you filed. Significant problems should not wait for discussion in a formal review. You don't want to approach the formal performance review with negative surprises. This documentation focuses on actual performance and experience rather than personality issues. As a result, you'll be more likely to remain objective.

1. Formulate positive behavior goals for your employee. During performance appraisals, it's easy to come from the negative point of view, i.e., listing the things that are not being done, etc. *It is better to ask for more of something than less of something.* Express yourself in terms of what is needed. Use a positive rather than a negative approach. For example, the statement "You are always late" needs to be changed to "You need to be on time." You may think it's a small change, but taken all together, such statements can send very powerful messages.

How Not to Do It

You are never on time.

How to Do It

You need to be here on time every day.

How Not to Do It

You're rigid.

How to Do It

You need to be more flexible.

How Not to Do It

You're too fussy.

How to Do It

You need to learn to distinguish between what's important and what's not important on the job.

---

2. Identify what's needed to improve the employee's performance. In what ways should he function more effectively? Determine whether addressing the problem is worth your time. If it's unimportant, you waste your time, the employee's time and the company's resources on an area where the return is not satisfactory. This is not good business.

3. Concentrate on the causes of the problem, not the symptoms. The solution must be related to the problem or it will be ineffective.

   Consult the following checklist:

   • Identify "nonperformance."

   • Determine if it is worth the time required to change nonperformance to performance.

   • Does the employee know that the performance is not satisfactory?

- Does the employee clearly understand what he is supposed to do and when?

- Are there any obstacles that are beyond the employee's control?

- Does the employee know how to do the job?

- Does a negative result occur if the employee does not perform?

- Have you removed rewards for your employee's nonperformance?

- Could the employee do the task if he wanted to?

4. Collect information without making judgments by talking to the employee. Then you can help him discover what to do differently so that the results will change. Remember, you must identify the *behavior* that is causing the problem.

5. Make sure the employee knows there is a problem. Identify both the *specific* behavior changes you want your employee to make and *what the employee would have to do to* convince you the problem has been solved.

How to Do It

Supervisor: *(Thinking)* Mark never listens, and he always seems to misunderstand directions. My goal is to have him listen and understand what I ask him to do. The specific things Mark will have to do to convince me he has accomplished this goal are:

- Do things the way I ask him to do them, unless he checks with me first.

- Ask me for clarification if he does not understand.

- Repeat back to me the instruction, confirming his understanding.

6. Identify success areas. You must know where the employee is performing effectively and provide *specific* examples in each area. This cannot be emphasized enough. It is important to show positive performance examples as well as negative ones. If necessary, identify the specific consequences that will occur if the employee does not take action.

7. Review background information. It is helpful to know the employee's length of service with the company, the current projects the employee is working on, the date of the employee's last promotion, the employee's educational and experiential background, etc.

In summary, don't sit down with your employee until you have covered each of the above areas using your performance log on that employee, a record of the employee's attendance, the employee's personnel file, the employee's job description, and the job and career objectives drawn up in your last performance appraisal with your employee as reference. Then you are prepared.

Defining Job Expectations

Earlier we touched on job descriptions and their importance to the appraisal process. In preparing for the appraisal, you must examine the existing job description. What is its focus in the following areas?

- Customer satisfaction

- Economic health of the company

- Innovation

- Quality

- Productivity

- Human resources

- Organizational climate

List your own job expectations. Decide what you really expect this person to do on the job in the areas of:

- Objectives

- Projects

- Authority

- Priority

- Scheduling

- Results/standards of performance

What things do *you* value the most?

Appraise performance, not expectations. What are the employee's major strengths and weaknesses? What personal characteristics or habits block greater achievement? What's ahead for this person? Why?

Thought must be given at this point to how each of the above areas will be addressed in the appraisal interview with the employee. If each area is addressed, will it be too much for the employee to handle in one sitting? Which areas are the most important and how will they be covered?

Be conscious of the following tendencies and try to avoid them as you prepare to assess your employee:

- *Trait Assessment*: Too much attention to certain characteristics that have nothing to do with the job or are difficult to measure blind us to more important traits.

- *Overemphasis*: Too much emphasis on favorable or unfavorable performance of one or two tasks could lead to an unbalanced evaluation of the overall employee contribution.

- *Bias/Prejudice*: Things that have nothing to do with performance such as race, religion, education, family background, age, handicapped status and/or gender do not belong in the evaluation.

- *False Reliance*: Relying on impressions rather than on facts is unfair.

- *Misplaced Accountability*: Holding the employee responsible for factors beyond his control is unrealistic.

Concentrate on performance measured against mutually understood expectations.

Asking the Employee to Meet — The Personal Touch

Your primary objective is to prepare the employee for a meaningful discussion with you. Don't have your secretary or another associate carry the invitation and don't send a memo. When you ask personally, you have control over the entire process. You don't have to worry about another layer complicating communications. The personal touch is an important component you want to capitalize on at this point, and you want to begin the entire interaction on a positive, personal note.

- Don't combine the meeting itself with the invitation. Give the employee time to organize his thoughts so his feedback is more helpful to the process. Without sufficient time to prepare, people are normally reactionary and can become resentful.

- Don't underinform or overinform your employee of the details needed for a successful meeting.

- Don't be ambiguous; be clear. Ambiguity can result in anxiety. Anxiety can be counterproductive to good communication.

- Don't say too much or get dragged into answering questions that should be part of the appraisal interview.

- Don't mock the process by making jokes. You'll lose your credibility and any hope of achieving worthwhile objectives.

- Don't arrange the meeting when you are upset or angry.

The best way to ask an employee to meet is to approach him privately. Explain the purpose of the meeting and how you would like him to prepare. This is very important. Suggest that the employee prepare for the meeting by thinking of things he is doing well and areas that need improvement. The employee should also be asked to come prepared to discuss:

1. Job performance issues since the last review

2. Personal career objectives

3. Problems or concerns about the present job

4. Goals for improving performance and productivity

Finally, ask the employee to think about things you can do to make things better. This also is important. It sends a message that you want to hear the employee's input. It shows that you think of the appraisal as a two-way street, that you and the employee are a team and that you'll do your part. You might want to photocopy the list on pages 47-48 as a tool your employee can use to prepare for his appraisal meeting.

How to Do It

Supervisor: *(To employee when no one is near)* I'd like to arrange a time to meet with you to review your work performance. Everyone in the office will be scheduled soon.

Employee: Okay …

Supervisor: I'm going to prepare for this meeting by writing down some of the things you have been doing really well and some of the areas where you can improve … I'd like you to prepare for the meeting by doing the same. First, think about the things you are doing well. Then concentrate on the areas where you feel you could improve.

Employee: I can do that.

Supervisor: Also, I'd like you to think about areas where I could help make your job less frustrating and more satisfying for you. Okay?

Employee: Really? … I'll work on it.

Supervisor: Good. How's next Monday at 10:00 a.m. in my office?

Employee: That will be just fine.

Supervisor: Good. I'll see you then.

Questions the employee can ask as he prepares for his performance appraisal:

- What critical abilities does my job require?

- What were my special accomplishments during this appraisal period?

- What do I like about my job? What don't I like?

- What goals or standards didn't I meet?

- How could my supervisor help me?

- Is there anything that the organization or my supervisor is doing that is hindering my progress?

- How can I become more productive?

- Do I need more experience or training in my current job?

- What have I done since my last appraisal to prepare myself for more responsibility?

- What new goals or standards should be applied for the next appraisal period? Which old ones should be discarded?

Get organized and rehearse each step if you feel it's necessary in order to set the stage for the positive appraisal to follow.

The Employee Self-Analysis

A well-done performance appraisal requires the collaboration of you and your employee. The first step is to understand why the employee's self-analysis is important. Employees will appreciate your interest in their analysis because it's an expression of interest in them. By listening to your employee's view of his performance, you'll see things from another perspective. The self-analysis involves the employee in the process and helps cement a strong relationship between you. You'll get a much clearer picture of any differences in viewpoint, and you'll get valuable new information on strengths and areas needing improvement.

Communicate to your employee that the purpose is to:

- List areas of major responsibility and accountability.

- Identify areas where the employee thinks he is performing effectively.

- Identify areas for improvement and some specific things he could do to show improvement in each area.

- Help your employee chart realistic goals for the future.

Let the employee know you will be going through these steps also and that you will be comparing notes.

How to Do It

Supervisor: *(Begin by asking your employee to share his self-analysis.)* Let's begin by talking about how you think you're doing on your job … I'd like you to start by telling me several things you think you do particularly well. Please give me specific examples.

Employee: Okay … *(Very unsure)*

Supervisor: For instance, if I were asked to do a self-analysis, I'd mention my skill at prioritizing the work for my employees. To give an example, I would say, "I am very direct in outlining work assignments and when I expect things to be done." Do you understand what I mean and can you do this for me?

Employee: Yes. I relate well to the customer. *(Pause)* I think I'm flexible. *(Pause)* I also think I'm good at responding quickly in emergency situations. *(Pause, looking serious and thoughtful)*

Supervisor: Good. I heard you mention three things. One, you're good at relating to the customers. Two, you're flexible. And three, you respond quickly in emergency situations. In what ways are you good at relating to customers? What are some of the things you do that lead you to conclude that this is a strong point?

How to Do It (Continued)

Employee: Many customers are fearful when they come here. They are expecting to have a lot of trouble getting their problems resolved. I try to change the situation to a positive one by becoming someone they can relate to when they're here. I try to make sure they understand I'm listening to their troubles, and I give them assurance that something will be done.

Supervisor: *(Pausing to make sure the employee is finished)* I see. You're good at relating to customers because you reduce the fearfulness of the situation by becoming their ally, letting them know you care that their problem is solved. Is that right?

Employee: Right. I think things like that are really important.

Supervisor: Very important. *(Pause)* Let's move to another area. You said you thought you were very good at emergencies. How did you mean that?

Employee: Do you remember the Davis case? There was a lot of tension in that situation. I wasn't nervous or scared during the entire episode.

Supervisor: Okay. Now let's identify several areas where you need to improve your work performance, those areas where you aren't performing as effectively as you might be. I'd like you to think about some of the specific things you'd actually do to improve in each area. *(Pause)* For example, one of the areas where I'd like to improve is handling conflicts between our department and other departments. One thing I know I could do to improve is to have the departments sit down together rather than meet with me one at a time. Do you understand?

How to Do It (Continued)

Employee: Don't you think you're in a better position to tell me what areas I need to improve? You're familiar with my work, and you're my boss!

Supervisor: Yes, but for now I'd like to get some of your thoughts. I'll give you my suggestions later.

Employee: Okay. Let's see. The biggest thing, and I know you'll agree because you've reminded me of it, has to do with the customer service reports. I definitely think I can improve by writing up those reports when I finish each project. Another thing has to do with being better about getting here on time, especially when we're near the end of the month. *(Smiling)*

Supervisor: Yes … *(Pause)* So two areas where you could improve are being more conscientious about writing up customer service reports and getting to work on time. Anything else?

Employee: No, I can't think of anything right now.

Supervisor: Let's start with the first area, writing up customer service reports. What are some specific things you'd do to improve your performance in this area?

Employee: *(Pause)* Well, I put them off until the last minute, and I usually end up scribbling my notes so they're hard for other people to read. *(Pause)* Because I'm rushing, I sometimes forget to record important information.

Supervisor: Okay, so to improve in this area, you'd have to take the time to write notes that are legible and more complete?

Employee: Right. If they were legible, complete and on time, I would definitely say I had improved in this area.

How to Do It (Continued)

Supervisor: *(Smiling)* All right. A little later, we'll talk about what you might actually do to achieve that goal. But now let's turn to the second area ... arriving on time. What do you need to do to improve in that area?

Employee: *(Smiling)* That's easy! Just get to work on time.

Supervisor: Okay. But could you be just a little more specific? For example, if you got to work on time every day for the next 10 days, would you say you had achieved your goal?

Employee: Oh ... I see what you mean. *(Pause)* Uh ... I guess now I arrive just a few minutes late about once a week. I guess I'd say that if I cut that down to being late only once a month, I'd have achieved the goal.

In this scenario, you see that a give-and-take, cooperative tone has been established, helping the employee look at both the positive and the negative aspects of performance.

1. Review each employee's job description. Does it truly reflect what you want that person to do? Are the expectations crystal clear ... or are there points of conflict or confusion within the job itself?

2. Modify the description as appropriate and review the changes in detail with the employee — specifically what is expected, when and how.

3. Set up a performance log for each employee.

Date	Event	Action	Result	Follow-up Information

   Update the log at least weekly, documenting each unusual event as well as factually summarizing overall performance on an ongoing basis.

4. Prepare for the performance review interview. Be sure to review the points on pages 40-42.

5. Ask the employee to complete a self-analysis using the questions on pages 47-48 as a guide.

6. Conduct the interview. Then critique yourself. What did you do well? What could you improve upon for the next one? How will you make the necessary adjustments?

Reflections

6 UNDERSTANDING MOTIVATION

What is motivation? Is it what you do to get others to do something you want them to do? Is it something that happens inside an individual that gets her to do something? The answer to both questions is "yes." In this chapter, we will explore various theories of motivation and how you can use this knowledge to improve performance in your organization.

Theories of Motivation

1. **Hierarchy of Needs.** One theory of motivation holds that humans direct their actions to satisfy their own needs. Once a need is satisfied, it no longer motivates. Abraham H. Maslow, an often quoted author on the subject, categorizes needs as follows:

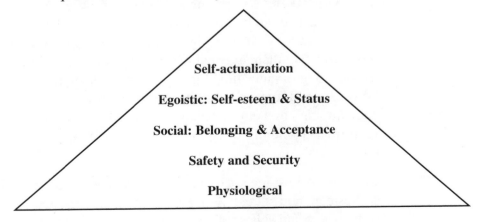

Self-actualization

Egoistic: Self-esteem & Status

Social: Belonging & Acceptance

Safety and Security

Physiological

- **Physiological:** At the lowest level are the physiological needs — food, air, water, etc. These needs, when satisfied, cease to be motivators of behavior. (When they are not met, however, the basic physiological needs become important to the exclusion of all else.)

- **Safety and Security:** When the physiological needs are met, needs at the next higher level begin to motivate behavior. These are needs for protection against danger, threat and deprivation.

  As long as we feel we are being treated fairly, our safety needs in the workplace will be satisfied. If we become uncertain and confused about management actions, we will feel insecure, and our safety needs will begin to dominate our behavior. Consider, for example, employees in an organization experiencing "downsizing." Most feel their safety and security are threatened by economic conditions. In these instances, a manager must move to address these issues head-on as any focus on higher level needs would be fruitless ... and viewed by the threatened employee as insincere.

- **Social:** Social needs become important motivators when physiological and security needs have been met. These include the need to belong, to associate with and be accepted by one's peers. Cohesive, tight-knit work groups may be far more effective than an equal number of separate individuals in achieving organizational goals. Management actions, however, tend to cause splinters in the cohesion by encouraging competitive behavior, rewarding individual performance and discouraging discussion among co-workers.

- **Egoistic:** Above the social needs live the ego needs, namely self-esteem and status. Self-esteem includes the need for self-respect and self-confidence, autonomy, competence and knowledge. Status needs include recognition, appreciation and the respect of others.

- **Self-actualization:** At the top of the pyramid are the needs for self-fulfillment. These are the needs for personal growth, self-development and for realizing one's potential.

Supervisors must determine at what level of need a particular employee is operating, and then ensure that elements in the workplace exist to satisfy those needs. Long conversations are often the way to understand what is going on in the employee's head. Ongoing reassessment is critical as individuals may change levels as circumstances around them change. The supervisor must then interact with each employee individually. A "one-size-fits-all" management strategy will not work.

2. **Theory X vs. Theory Y**

Another way of looking at employee motivation is Theory X versus Theory Y, a concept advanced by Douglas McGregor. Theory X assumes that people:

- Hate work

- Are not ambitious

- Are not responsible

- Prefer to be told what to do

Theory X managers believe that people work only as long as they are watched, must be told specifically what to do and how to do it, and must be closely controlled until they do it.

Theory Y assumes that the average human learns to not only accept responsibility, but to seek it. Commitment to objectives is a function of the rewards associated with their achievement. Many people have a high degree of imagination, ingenuity and creativity. Workers can be self-directed in the pursuit of the organization's objectives.

Theory Y managers believe that positive results can be achieved by setting up conditions that allow for achievement, including the creation of the right atmosphere. If a manager finds that her employees are lazy, indifferent, unwilling to take responsibility and uncooperative, Theory Y implies that the causes lie in management's methods of organization and control.

3. **Satisfaction and Dissatisfaction Factors.** Another noted behavior scientist, Frederick Herzberg, performed research on motivation, identifying satisfaction and dissatisfaction factors among workers. He found achievement to be the strongest employee motivator. Small achievements act as motivators, which cause people to achieve even more. According to Herzberg, the second strongest motivator is recognition. One effective way to increase productivity, for example, is to provide opportunities for achievement, giving the supervisor more opportunities to reward and recognize.

What Employees Want

- Good working conditions

- To feel "in" on things

- A fair discipline system

- Full appreciation of their contributions

- Recognition and feedback from co-workers, supervisors and customers

- Equitable wages

- Opportunity for growth

- Empathy with personal problems

- Job security

- Challenging work

- To know management genuinely cares

Unfortunately, most supervisors spend a lot of time convincing employees that the good work they produce is normal — that what they achieve is somehow expected and what they are paid to do! Recognition takes numerous forms beyond raises, bonuses or promotions. A major form of recognition is the positive things managers say to their achieving employees! Good supervision is recognizing the runners in the race who haven't won but are running better than they did before. So what can you do?

- Get out from behind your desk so you can discover more occurrences of achievement. Catch your employees doing something good.

- Recognize achievement immediately, the minute you become aware of it.

- Acknowledge that lesser degrees of failure are achievements; recognize them. Reward effort.

- Find more ways to show appreciation. Expressing thanks is a neglected form of compensation.

Become a Leadership Role Model

- Learn all you can about how to motivate peak performance.

- Take total responsibility for your own performance and teach this modus operandi to others.

- Help your people get a fair share of the action.

- Understand and model self-motivation.

- Give your people sufficient reasons to want to excel.

- See yourself in a service capacity dedicated to helping others perform at peak levels.

- Offer special assistance to standard performers but stay out of the way of peak performers unless they ask for help.

1. Assess the need level of each of your employees based on Maslow's hierarchy as presented on page 55.

    • Where is each right now?

    • What can you do to meet those needs?

    • Establish a schedule in which you take a few moments to formally reassess each employee's need level.

2. In reviewing your management style, identify whether you are a Theory X or Theory Y manager. What steps can you take to strengthen your Theory Y attitude and approach to your people?

3. Identify two ways you can implement each of the following and commit yourself to action. (Continue on the next page.)

Reflections

Get out from behind your desk so you can discover more occurrences of achievement.

Activity/Idea   **Implementation Date**

Catch your employees doing something good.

    1.

    2.

Give instant recognition.

    1.

    2.

Reward effort.

    1.

    2.

Show your appreciation.

    1.

    2.

Reflections

7 THE PERFORMANCE APPRAISAL FACE-TO-FACE

You've already done the hardest part; you've begun the process by committing to deal with the employee, and you've set the time and place. Your objective now is to begin the interview so that you *maximize the employee's participation*. In this chapter, we will look more closely at the techniques to get into the heart of the interview and discuss the employee's self-analysis.

Building Employee Participation

Be sure you do not begin a performance appraisal until you are in control of the issues and your emotions. Before the meeting, decide the minimum action you will consider acceptable, what alternative solutions are available, and when you expect performance to improve.

Set the stage by minimizing distractions and interruptions. Clear your desk and your mind of everything unrelated to the current situation. Hold the calls and close the door. Make sure you have read all the necessary paperwork and that it is at your disposal.

Make sure the temperature in the room is comfortable, water is available, and that the employee will be seated in a comfortable chair. Make the employee, not the appraisal form, the center of your focus. Make sure to allow enough time for the meeting so you don't have to end the discussion before it's completed.

You can make the person feel comfortable and welcome by beginning with a little casual conversation to get things started, but do not spend too much time on this. Sit face-to-face with no desk in between you if possible. This way, your body language will send the message that you're both on the same team, both trying to solve a common problem.

Structure the meeting by using a topical agenda, a brief order of events, so the employee knows what to expect. Begin by explaining why you are meeting and what is planned. Make sure the employee knows that every employee will participate in one of these meetings. It's part of your job and theirs. Also, make sure the employee understands that you will not be talking about money issues, that another meeting will be set up for that purpose. Instead, the focus is to talk about job performance and setting objectives for the future.

Explain that you are going to do the following:

- Find out how things are going in general.

- Ask the employee to explain how you can help make things better.

- Review the objectives of the job and the job description.

- Listen carefully to the employee's self-rating.

- Offer your own rating of the employee's strengths and weaknesses. Form a general impression of competence.

- Mutually agree on future goals for the employee.

Handling Employee Questions

Answer any question the employee may have at any time during this explanation. Acknowledge the question and the feeling behind it. Let the employee know you understand. Respond directly to the concern. Get the employee's reaction. Make sure you've addressed the employee's concern before you move on.

Understand the types of questions employees have. Questions usually take one of the following shapes:

- *Hostile questions* such as, "Why do I have to be first?" or "Boy, are we going to talk about things you need to do, because there sure are a lot of them." These types of questions usually indicate the person is feeling threatened or angry about having to talk to you. Reflect the person's feeling by asking for more information until the employee has had a chance to vent his hostility, then move on to the heart of the interview.

- *Neutral questions* such as, "How long will this meeting take?" or "What do you mean by 'goals'?" These are clarifying questions. Your employee is unclear. Keep your responses simple. Answer as honestly and directly as you can and then move on.

- *Questions of concern* such as, "Will anyone else know what we talk about in this meeting?" or "Will all this go in my personnel record?" Your response needs to show that you understand the employee's feeling. Again, answer as honestly and directly as you can before moving on.

How to Do It

Supervisor: Come in and sit down. Please relax. The purpose of this meeting is to evaluate your performance and for us to work out together the best path for your future. Have you brought the forms I asked you to fill out for today's meeting?

Employee: Yes, I have.

Supervisor: Excellent. I've filled out the same forms. I want to compare what we've written on these forms so we can see where we agree and disagree. You placed a great deal of emphasis on product changes, much more than I would.

Employee: Really? I enjoy that part of my job.

Supervisor: I really need your talents used in other areas. In fact, I'd like to see your time commitment changed by the next time we meet. Tell me, why do you think you spend so much time on product changes?

Employee: I think it's because the people in Department B are always coming to me with bits and pieces of things they want me to do or want me to change. Maybe we need better communication.

Supervisor: That's a good thought. I'll talk to the supervisor of Department B. Maybe we can get something more productive worked out.

This scenario started with a comfortable opening and then set a direct path to discussing what was on the supervisor's mind. With some employees, you will need to spend more time on finding out how things are going, as we'll see on the following pages.

Finding Out How Things Are Going

It's important to explore what's on the mind of your employee, thereby opening the door to mutual understanding. This sends a signal to your employee that you care about what he has to say, which is good for morale. It also clears the air for discussions to follow by giving the employee a chance to talk about his problems and concerns. This can be an early warning system! You gain perspective. By listening early, you build a give-and-take rapport with the employee that will be useful later. Remember, you are asking your employee to talk about his favorite topic ... himself.

How to Do It

Supervisor: *(Leaning forward slightly)* How are things going for you here at ABC Company in general?

Employee: Well, I guess things are going pretty well for the most part. That's a little tough to answer all at once ... I really don't know where to begin.

Supervisor: *(Nodding and smiling)* Yes, I understand. Take your time. I'm very interested in what you have to say.

Employee: Let's see. Things have been going pretty well. I like it here much more than my last job in Company B. I love my job. The atmosphere's a lot more relaxed, and people seem to enjoy what they do.

Supervisor: *(Nodding)* Yes ...

Employee: Well, I guess — oh! ... the bonuses! Thank goodness for the bonuses! *(Smiling broadly)*

Supervisor: *(Smiling back)* Sounds as if you're pretty happy about the bonuses.

Employee: Am I ever! My daughter is in college, and boy, do those bonuses help!

How to Do It (Continued)

Supervisor: Good, I'm glad you feel that way. Now, I'd like to hear about anything you don't like or any problems you've been having on the job.

Employee: Problems? *(Looking down and hesitating)* Ah … Well, for one thing, the workload gets fairly heavy sometimes, and I have a little trouble keeping up. All the managers act as if their work is the most important. They expect me to do everything "right now." And they get pretty upset if they don't get what they want right away.

Supervisor: *(Nodding)* I imagine that is difficult.

Employee: They have no knowledge of the work the other managers have already given me, and they don't seem to care about anything except their own work.

Supervisor: So you really feel major pressure at those times?

Employee: Sometimes I feel so tense I just want to run away. I don't know how to handle it. And then I start making mistakes. And that makes more work to correct, and I'm further behind!

Supervisor: I'm glad you told me about it. And I think there are a number of things we might do. *(Pause)* But let's talk about solutions to that problem a little later. I'd like to hear about any other problems you have before we get too deeply into solutions. I want to make sure I understand everything that is bothering you.

Employee: Okay. Well … *(Pause)* There is … *(Pause)* it's, uh *(Pause)* *(Much hesitation)* Susan … *(Pause)*

Supervisor: Susan?

How to Do It (Continued)

Employee: I don't want to get anyone in trouble, but she can be very difficult at times.

Supervisor: When you say "difficult," how do you mean it?

Employee: It's related to the workload problem. We're supposed to help each other when the crunch is on. I'll ask her for some help, and she'll say that she's busy, but then she seems to find the time to gab for a half-hour on the telephone while I'm breaking my neck to keep the managers off my back.

Supervisor: So you get pretty annoyed when she does that?

Employee: You bet! I guess I never realized how much I let it get to me. I've never said anything about it to her.

Supervisor: Okay, it sounds as if your main problems have to do with the workload, the pressure you feel from the managers, the mistakes that come from that situation, and Susan's unwillingness to help out when the crunch is on. Is that correct?

Employee: *(Nodding)* Right. And those really are big problems!

Supervisor: Yes, they are, and a little later, we'll talk about some ways to deal with them. But now I'd like to move on to another subject. I'd like you to think about some ways I could make your job a little less frustrating and more satisfying for you. What ideas or suggestions do you have along those lines?

Employee: Let me see. Well, one thing is … I'd really like to know more about what everybody does around here.

Supervisor: So, you'd like to find out more about the nature of their jobs and how they fit into the big picture?

How to Do It (Continued)

Employee: Yes.

Supervisor: What else can I do to make things less frustrating and more satisfying for you?

Employee: The computers in our department keep breaking down, and it always seems to be when we have deadlines.

Supervisor: Based on everything you've said so far, I need to work on four things to make life more satisfying and enjoyable for you around here. First, I need to speak to the managers about the workload problem. Maybe I can help them set up some kind of priority system so you don't get hit all at once with everything.

Second, I may have to speak with Susan about being more cooperative when the crunch is on.

Employee: *(Nervously)* Are you sure that's a good idea? Will she know we talked? I don't want her thinking I'm a rat.

Supervisor: I can appreciate that. But, believe me, I won't handle it that way. As I said when I asked you to meet with me, I'll be doing this sort of thing with everybody.

Employee: Okay.

Supervisor: Third, I think it would be a good idea if I arranged for you to meet some of the other people in the department so you can understand the roles they play.

Employee: I'd like that.

Supervisor: Great! And then fourth, I need to have the computers looked at. Okay, I'd like to move on to another topic, your work performance.

Before you begin your performance appraisal, recognize that discussing employee performance is where you are most likely to encounter initial resistance. Identifying problem behavior patterns helps set the stage for effective action.

One of the major types of problem behaviors is hostility. Hostile people bully or even overwhelm others. Usually, they make critical remarks. Give the hostile employee time to run down. Don't answer shouting with shouting. Get him to sit down and keep eye contact. State your own opinions firmly and don't act frightened. Stand up to him without fighting. If the shouting continues, ask the employee to leave and come back when he has calmed down.

How to Do It

Employee: *(Agitated)* I tell you, some changes better get made at this company soon, or a lot of people are going to quit. And - I'm not the only one who'll tell you that!

Supervisor: I hear a lot of anger in your voice. *(Leaning forward slightly)* I'd like to hear how you're feeling.

Employee: *(Slightly startled)* Well, I am really angry! I don't know whose fault it is, but we don't get much management. We're left on our own to make key decisions, and then we're criticized for making the wrong ones! Everyone around here thinks the quality of management in this company leaves much to be desired!

Supervisor: *(Looking directly into the employee's eyes)* Sounds as if your anger has a lot to do with the direct supervision you're getting … or maybe that you're not getting. Isn't that anger really directed at me?

Employee: *(A little flustered)* I … didn't mean anything about you personally. Well … uh, that's not true either. It does have something to do with you.

How to Do It (Continued)

Supervisor: I really want to hear what's on your mind, even if it is critical of me. Level with me and be as direct as you can. *(Puts down pen and faces employee, giving full attention)* What suggestions do you have for how I could improve the way I supervise?

Employee: Sometimes you give me a lot of work to do without telling me why I should do it. I waste a lot of my time doing things for no purpose at all. It makes me feel like I'm not important enough for you to take the time to make sure I understand. And usually there is no priority assigned to the work, so I'm never sure where I should start.

Supervisor: So one thing I could do is explain the purpose of the work I assign to you, giving a better idea of why I want it done, why it's important and what priority it has?

Employee: That would help a lot. A whole lot. And there are some other things ... if you're sure you'd like to hear them. *(Smiling)*

Supervisor: *(Smiling)* I would like to hear them. Go ahead ...

Often critical remarks are rooted in anger, resulting in hostility. In this scenario, you can see how the supervisor allowed the employee to vent his feelings and then directed the conversation productively. Let's continue to learn from this exchange.

How to Do It

Supervisor: You've been very honest with me, so I think I've got a pretty good idea about some of your problems. I'd like to wait to talk about solutions until a little later …

Employee: (*Interrupting*) What do you mean "wait to talk about solutions" until later? What's the sense of identifying problems if you don't want to talk about them? I just told you how upset I am, and now you don't want to talk about how to solve the problems?

Supervisor: You're angry and irritated that I changed the subject before talking about solutions, is that right? (*Reflecting feeling*)

Employee: Yeah! I mean, it just doesn't make any sense. This whole thing is beginning to feel like a total waste of time.

Supervisor: You're saying that you want to talk about solutions right now, not after we've discussed anything else.

Employee: That's exactly what I'm saying, and I mean it!

Supervisor: I also think talking about solutions to the problems you mentioned is very important. I plan to spend a lot of time later in this interview to do just that, but I want to talk about some other things first. I'd like to hear your suggestions for how I could make your job more satisfying, and we need to do a thorough review of your work performance.

Employee: Well, I think it's more important to talk about solutions while the problems are still fresh in our minds.

How to Do It (Continued)

Supervisor: Let's step back from this for just a minute to get a fresh perspective. It seems we disagree on how to proceed. You'd like to discuss solutions to some of the problems you identified right now. You feel they're important, and you want to get them solved. I do too, but I'd like to talk about solutions after we've covered some other areas so I have a good understanding of the total picture. I'd like to find a way out of this disagreement, preferably with a solution that we both can live with so we can get on with improving things for both of us. What do you think is our next step?

Employee: *(Pauses while thinking)* I don't really know. *(Smiling)* We can always do it my way … *(Laughing)* Well, we can maybe spend a few minutes talking about solutions to the things I told you were big problems to me. Then, if it looks as if we're not going to come up with any real solutions very quickly, or if we have more to talk about, we can talk about it again later in the interview.

Supervisor: Very good idea. Suppose we spend 15 minutes now talking about some potential solutions?

You can see how the emotion was controlled while a compromise evolved. The employee in this situation felt he was being heard and was playing an active role in the interview. This sort of feeling lays the groundwork for true communication.

Problem Behavior and What to Do in a Performance Appraisal

There are other types of behavior problems besides hostility.

Complainers are people who gripe incessantly but never do anything about their problems. With these people,

1. Listen.

2. Acknowledge their feelings. Feelings are always valid.

3. Paraphrase the facts.

4. Move to problem-solving.

Unresponsive people respond only with yes/no answers or silence. Ask open-ended questions and wait patiently. Lean slightly toward the employee, using body language to show your interest, and inform the employee of what he must do to put the problem behind him.

Too agreeable people, while being very supportive, rarely produce what they say they will, or they act contrary to the way you have been led to expect. Bring to the surface the underlying facts and ask for their feedback, especially negative. Be prepared to move toward action, expectations and deadlines.

Negative people always respond with comments like, "It won't work." Your task is to present often optimistic but realistic statements about past successes while making sure the problem is thoroughly discussed both positively and negatively. Highly analytical people need sufficient time before you can expect them to act positively, avoiding negative tendencies.

Know-it-alls appear as condescending, pompous, imposing people who sometimes really are experts. Make sure you prepare yourself well before meeting with the "know-it-all." Structure your questions toward facts and then raise problems. Ask "what-if" questions to assist in re-examining your concerns.

Stallers slow down their decision-making until others make a decision for them. They have trouble letting go of anything until everything is perfect, which it never is. You must make it easy for stallers to tell you about conflicts or reservations that prevent their decisions. Listen for indirect clues that may provide insight into problem areas and give support after a decision is made. Try to keep any action steps as your responsibility.

Criers have problems controlling their emotions, and the tears show it. Often they are as embarrassed and as uncomfortable as you are. You can leave the room and let the employee gain composure, but identify the discomfort both of you are feeling as you leave.

Any of these behaviors can cause difficulty during a performance appraisal. When an employee refuses to go along with the game plan, you can use the Stop-Look-Listen approach.

Stop-Look-Listen Approach

Stop the interaction before it becomes argumentative or unproductive.

- Don't get angry.

- Don't get defensive.

- Don't blame others.

- Don't lecture.

Look squarely at the problem and describe it succinctly to the employee.

Listen for suggestions and ways to resolve the problem together.

Another problem can arise when an employee talks too much. When this happens, decrease the use of verbal and nonverbal encouragement. That is, don't smile and nod as much. You can also cut down on direct eye contact.

Close the subject. Move to a new topic by setting time limits and reminding the employee of all that must be discussed. Reward concise answers with positive feedback.

Asking Your Employee How You Can Help

You may think you don't want to ask how you can help because:

- It's threatening.

- You expect the worst.

- You think the employee should ask the question, not you.

You *should* ask this question because:

- Employees love it.

- It gives you feedback on how you're doing as a boss.

- You'll begin to hear common themes.

- You'll gain perspective.

- It may unlock the door to increased performance.

- It lays the groundwork for creating performance agreement.

One of your objectives during the performance appraisal is to use your experience by adding to the alternatives your employee has to select from when faced with making a decision. Your employee may not see what you see, so help him.

Ten Things to Improve Employee Performance

1. Provide current information about the organization — even if it is not good news.

2. Define the group's goals.

3. Define what is expected of individual employees.

4. Be clear about relationships with other groups.

5. Give immediate recognition of good performance.

6. Give immediate attention to important mistakes.

7. Have a development plan for each person.

8. Balance rewards and results.

9. Reward group achievement when possible.

10. Build listening time into your schedule.

Setting the Course for Action

Now comes the actual work of unifying all the elements into a constructive outcome by appraising performance and communicating the appraisal successfully to your employee.

The performance appraisal is a summary of your work observations. After each key area of accountability in your employee's job description is evaluated, his overall performance is evaluated. The results are summarized on the next page.

Let's look at each one of these areas by beginning with unsatisfactory performance. There are two types — correctable and uncorrectable. "What is influencing poor performance?" is the most important question to ask yourself in contemplating how to correct unsatisfactory performance.

Consult your performance log. If you built your log correctly, then after you observed a performance discrepancy, you should have collected valid information on your employee's performance and included them in the log from the onset. This eliminates surprises later. Your analysis of nonperformance should reveal trends. If there are no trends, you may have observed a simple blip that's minimally worth pursuing. If there are trends, the formal, sit-down performance appraisal session is the place to address performance concerns.

You must be extremely careful when determining the reasons for nonperformance. What originally got your attention was a symptom of nonperformance, not the cause. You must make sure the employee knows precisely what he is to do so that his behavior can change. For you to effectively monitor and help the employee change, you must know precisely what the behavior or the problem is. Your performance log will help you with this. It will also help you determine if the employee knows that his performance is not what it should be. Direct, specific questions should be asked on a day-to-day basis to clarify your log entries. Here are two questions you should learn to ask:

- "Do you know what your error rate is?"

- "Do you know how many days you arrived late for work in the last two weeks?"

Also, look at your internal support systems. Feedback should not always have to pass through you to get to the employee. One of today's management goals is empowered workers!

Following is a listing of common reasons why employees don't do what they're supposed to do. Use these potential reasons to organize yourself.

What's causing the problem?

_____ Not knowing what he is supposed to do

_____ Not knowing how to do it

_____ Not knowing why he should do it

_____ Fear of future negative consequences

_____ Experiencing personal problems

_____ Not recognizing personal limits

_____ Perceiving obstacles beyond his control

_____ Thinking your way will not work

_____ Thinking his way is better

_____ Thinking something else is more important

_____ Assuming no one could do it

_____ Thinking he is already doing it

_____ Being rewarded for not doing it

_____ Receiving no negative consequence for performing poorly

Remember, your employees must know exactly what you want in order to supply it and must know exactly what the consequences will be if they don't. That's where your careful analysis of each employee's job description and your discussion of job duties, expectations and consequences come into play. We will discuss preparation shortly.

Ask yourself if your objectives in this performance appraisal should be limited. Is there a limit to how much criticism your employee can absorb in one session? It may be too much to expect performance improvements in multiple areas within six months or even one year. However, you should know what improvements can be made and then gain the commitment from the employee to make them.

If you must select limited objectives, ask yourself the following questions:

- Which deficiencies are most critical to the company?

- Does the employee possess the confidence necessary to make the multiple changes?

- Can improvements be continuous, i.e., spread out over the calendar year rather than tackled all at once?

Plan how you are going to help the employee accept the need to improve. Compliance does not necessarily mean acceptance, and the best results come from acceptance, from the employee stating that improvement is needed.

How much improvement is enough?

- Get the employee to commit to a specific plan for improvement.

- Distinguish between improvement and correction. Correction is the overall goal. Improvement is progress in the right direction.

If the performance remains unsatisfactory or is not correctable, or if the person lacks the capacity or the desire to improve, you have some options. You can continue to tolerate the unsatisfactory performance or begin a termination interview, no longer focusing on appraisal. Consult with the personnel department or your boss for information on how to proceed. Remember, once you decide an employee's nonperformance is occurring because of some unchangeable limitation, you have closed the door to other alternatives. You are no longer managing that employee, and you can only watch what happens.

Now, let's look at the employee who has satisfactory performance but has no chance of promotion. There are two types of people here ... those who already know and accept the low probability of promotion and those who either don't know it or don't accept it. Every organization has people who should be promoted but won't be. These people are sometimes referred to as having "plateaued."

Those who don't accept their low probability of promotion will either rise, possibly in another company, or they will cause you problems.

Good performance does not, for many reasons, always ensure promotion. For employees for whom there is no promotion ahead, you must define the employee's objectives clearly. Focus on these issues:

- What will sustain this employee's current performance? This type of employee will have a large need for positive reinforcement.

- What will motivate this employee? This question must be answered in terms of the person's immediate unmet needs.

- What specific motivators would be effective with this employee? Delegate often to him, transferring your authority where possible.

- How can you provide job enrichment, stretching his job to offer greater challenges? Different from delegation, such changes are permanent and can come from others' work as well as your own.

- Is it possible to encourage participation, giving a larger share in decision-making?

- Is this employee capable of being involved in mentoring other employees? Recognize that transferring knowledge is an important contribution to the success of the company.

Some employees don't realize there is no promotion ahead for them. They need to know their position clearly.

- Hold the conversation in a favorable appraisal setting. Be supportive, explaining the outcome gently, and then look for ways to truly discuss the job at hand.

- Try to identify possible blockages while admitting that you don't have all the answers or control the promotion process.

By comparison, the interview for employees whose performance is satisfactory and for whom promotion lies ahead becomes a development interview, although promotion should not be guaranteed.

Your objective here is to shift the emphasis from present performance to preparation for a future job. Stress that development for the employee's next job does not overshadow the need to maintain satisfactory performance on his current job but that the new duties will supplement it. Verify realistic employee career plans and together build the plan for the future.

Possible development actions include:

- On-the-job development

- Personal coaching

- Planned exposure to new positions or duties

- In-house or off-the-job development

- Workshops, seminars, conferences

- Self-development and self-study

- College courses and advanced degrees

You can consult the following general performance guidelines when you talk to your employee, whether the employee is performing satisfactorily or not, is promotable or not:

- Use your log and appraisal form as a guide only.

- Start with the positive.

- Establish as much agreement as you can between your analysis and the employee's analysis.

- Be ready to shift from talking to listening.

- Get your employee's reaction to your analysis.

- Give direction after the employee reacts to your appraisal.

- Don't promise anything you can't deliver.

How to Do It

Supervisor: *(Nodding and then pausing for several seconds before speaking)* Anything else you want to add?

Employee: I really think that pretty much covers all the areas I wanted to talk about today.

Supervisor: Good. You provided me with a very complete and thoughtful analysis of your job performance and how things are going for you. You really seemed to get into it!

Employee: *(Smiling and obviously pleased)* Yes, I did.

Supervisor: Now, as I mentioned a little earlier, I'd like to add a few things to what you've said.

Employee: This is the part I've been dreading …

Supervisor: You're a little concerned about what I have to say about your performance?

Employee: Yes … as well as this seems to be going, I guess I am a little apprehensive. It isn't always the easiest thing to have somebody give you honest and objective feedback on how you're doing on your job. You're afraid to hear some things. You know they are probably true, but it's hard to face them. Especially, when it comes from your boss.

Supervisor: *(Nodding and smiling but saying nothing)*

Employee: That's all I was thinking … I guess I'm ready to listen … *(Leaning forward slightly)*

Supervisor: *(Smiling)* I asked you to start with the areas where you think you're performing well. I'd like to do the same thing.

Employee: *(Smiling)* Good … I don't mind starting there!

How to Do It (Continued)

Supervisor: One of the areas where you felt you were performing effectively was in making presentations. I'm in full agreement with that. Three of our most demanding managers have told me that you make excellent presentations, and they don't hand out compliments easily.

Employee: *(Smiling and looking a little embarrassed)* That's nice to know.

Supervisor: Yes, it is nice. Another thing, our training department has asked if they could use you as an instructor for new employee training.

Employee: *(A little surprised)* I didn't know that. I am really interested in being able to do that …

Supervisor: I'm glad. Let's talk about that in more detail later.

Employee: I'm looking forward to it!

Supervisor: Another area that you mentioned you were doing pretty well in is following up on leads the salespeople give you. Again, I'm in full agreement.

Employee: *(Nodding)*

Supervisor: At least three of our customers have told me they would never have considered, much less chosen, our line if it hadn't been for your persistent follow-up. That's exactly what we want our inside salespeople to do.

Employee: *(Smiling)* I hope they weren't saying I was bugging them too much.

Supervisor: Now, I'd like to talk about some areas that you didn't mention where I think you're performing effectively.

How to Do It (Continued)

Employee: *(Smiling and leaning forward a little)* Okay, that won't be hard to listen to …

Supervisor: A lot of the things you do around here have a motivating, almost inspirational, effect on others. Ever since we've been working together, I've noticed you're always trying to help the people here.

Employee: *(Smiling and nodding)* Yes, well, I would want someone to do that for me. I just do what's right.

Supervisor: *(Smiling and nodding)* I think "helpful" is a good way to characterize what you do. Let's talk about another area where I think you're performing effectively on the job. In fact, it's an area in which I think you could stand to improve. *(Pause)* I'd like to explain my thinking and get your reactions. And finally, I'd like us to reach some agreement on what you could work on to improve your performance over the next couple of months. *(Pause)*

Employee: Okay.

Supervisor: And after that, I'd like us to agree on what I'm going to do to help you improve in these areas.

Employee: Sounds good.

Supervisor: One area where I think you could improve is in handling objections.

Employee: *(Wrinkling forehead)* Handling objections? I disagree. I think I'm good at handling objections. In fact, I even keep a notebook on objections so I can come up with better and better arguments. I practice delivering responses to objections so I can deliver them with confidence.

How to Do It (Continued)

Supervisor: When a prospect offers an objection, such as it's too expensive or it's not compatible without other equipment, it's awfully tempting to come back with an argument to overcome the objection.

Employee: *(Nodding)* Absolutely.

Supervisor: But often the best thing to do is to get more information, draw the guy out. You want to get him talking.

Employee: If I draw him out, I would know more about what's bothering him and what he really thinks is important, what he really wants.

Supervisor: It seems you're willing to consider that as a possible strategy for handling objections? I admire that about you. You are always looking for ways to improve. Why don't we move on to another area? A second area I'd like to see some improvement in is meeting deadlines.

Employee: *(Shaking his head and smiling)* I knew those reports were going to creep into this conversation. I hate those reports, and you know it. They're a big waste of time. I'd rather be selling.

Supervisor: Sounds as if you find the reports unpleasant, almost as though they are an obstacle to getting more important things done? *(Reflecting feeling)*

Employee: *(Sighing)* Yes, that's just how I feel. I wish we could automate the process so the data would just be there as we made our calls.

Supervisor: I'm not big on paperwork either. On the other hand, if those reports don't get in on time, it causes lots of problems. Until we computerize the department, we're just going to have to do those reports. *(Pause)* Maybe at this point it would be helpful if you reviewed for both of

Finalizing Performance Improvement Plans

At this point in the review, you will identify:

- Specific tasks the employee is going to work on within a defined time frame

- Specific tasks you are going to work on during the same time frame to help the employee improve performance, removing frustrations and roadblocks

The next step is to develop a written record designed to help both of you keep the agreement. It contains these items:

- Specific tasks the employee can work on to improve his performance

- Specific tasks for you to work on that will assist and support your employee

- Specific tasks that will make the employee's job less frustrating and more satisfying while building for the future

The list of specific tasks you compile needs to be prioritized. It should contain short- and long-term objectives. Develop a plan of action that can be broken down into meaningful and achievable steps.

Use the following strategy:

- Ask what the employee would like to work on.

- Make additional suggestions on what you would like the employee to work on.

- Reach agreement on exactly what the employee will do first.

- Ask what you can do to help.

- Make additional suggestions, if necessary, on things the employee can accomplish.

- Reach agreement on exactly what will be done by you and when it will be done.

- Write it down.

How to Do It

Supervisor: Why don't you take a few minutes to talk about the specific things that you'd like to be working on over the next several weeks, given all the things that we've talked about so far?

Employee: Maybe I ought to put the worst first. Once I get that under control, the rest will be much easier. I'll make a commitment to get those monthly reports in on time every month for …

Supervisor: Say the next three months?

Employee: That sounds reasonable.

Supervisor: Great. What else? *(Beginning to make some notes)*

Employee: Well … I would like to work on learning new products.

Supervisor: *(Nodding and making more notes)* We've decided on getting your monthly reports in on time for the next three months and working on new products.

Employee: I still would like to do a better job of getting interviews with prospects. But I'll need some help in critiquing how I'm doing it now. Perhaps if we could spend some time role playing, I could get better at it.

Supervisor: *(Nodding)* Okay. Sounds good. Anything else?

Employee: I think that about covers it. I can't think of anything else.

Supervisor: *(Glancing at his notes)* You mentioned getting all your monthly reports in on time for the next three months, learning new products, and doing a better job of getting interviews. Does that pretty much cover it?

Employee: Yes.

Supervisor: Before we actually write down the tasks, I'd like to add a couple of ideas. Then we'll pare down the list to a manageable size.

The interview would proceed with the supervisor and employee listing all the areas needing work, setting reasonable dates for things to be done, and discussing all the ways the supervisor can help the employee achieve the objective.

Closing the Performance Appraisal Interview

In closing the review, ask for your employee's reaction.

- If an employee seems angry, agitated or upset, devote time to talking about these feelings.

- Help the employee come up with a solution to the problem.

- If you have different ideas on how to proceed, use the Stop-Look-Listen approach outlined earlier.

Share your reaction to the performance interview with your employee. If you are pleased, share your positive feelings. If you are not pleased, be honest without being brutal. Don't put the blame for what happened entirely on the employee. Try to stress the positive. Describe the specific problems briefly and objectively. Ask for suggestions on how the problem can be solved or avoided in future meetings, trying to reach a win-win status.

Schedule the follow-up meeting and end on a positive note. Walk the employee out in a friendly manner. Thank the employee and tell him you are looking forward to the follow-up meeting.

1. Do you enjoy conducting performance appraisals?

2. Do you enjoy receiving performance appraisals?

3. Do your employees regularly get feedback on their performance from their customers?

4. Are performance evaluations based on evidence of results?

5. Is performance evaluation information continuous throughout the year?

6. Does the performance feedback help the employee make improvements?

7. Are you required to have a distribution of ratings (e.g., not all can be outstanding)?

8. Does the performance information frequently get used as a guide to future action?

9. Are all employees in your department motivated with the same incentives?

10. Do your employees see you as a mentor or as a judge during performance review time?

Reflections

8 IMPROVING PERFORMANCE APPRAISAL INTERVIEWING SKILLS

Appraisal interviewing is a science. You can acquire the skills that can help you relate constructively and communicate more successfully with every employee. These essential skills and the most common appraisal pitfalls are discussed in this chapter.

Common Pitfalls

- **Fear of failure:** Many appraisers think they have a vested interest in making their subordinates look good on paper. They fear poor performance by a subordinate reflects poorly on the manager as well. Appraisers may fear possible repercussions — for themselves and their employee — if the organizational culture is intolerant of failure.

- **The "fudge factor":** Surveys show that many managers actually defend fudging as a tactic necessary for effective management. Some claim an overly generous appraisal can motivate a marginal performer to improve. Others fudge to hide difficulties from senior managers.

- **Aversion to judging:** Many people are reluctant to judge others and create a permanent record that may affect an employee's future. Training in constructive evaluation techniques may help. Appraisers need to recognize that problems not addressed can ultimately cause more harm than documentation of corrective action taken now.

- **Positive feedback-seeking game:** A poor performing employee regularly seeks informal praise from the supervisor at inappropriate moments. Often the feedback seeker will get the praise they want by ambushing the supervisor by seeking feedback when the supervisor is unable or unprepared to give them a full and proper answer … or in settings that are inappropriate for a candid assessment. This places the supervisor in a difficult situation when the formal review focuses on the employee's poor performance … and the employee recalls, with perfect clarity, every casual word of praise received.

- **Inadequate appraiser preparation:** Beware of the appraiser who wants to play it by ear. Such attitudes must be actively discouraged by stressing the importance and technical challenge of good performance appraisal.

- **Lack of employee participation:** Employees who participate with their supervisors in creating their own performance goals and development plans are more likely to truly commit to the plan. Mutual agreement is a key to success.

- **Isolated, year-end reviews:** One of the most common mistakes is to view the appraisal as an isolated event rather than an ongoing process. Frequent mini-appraisals and feedback sessions will help ensure that employees receive the ongoing guidance, support and encouragement they need. If appraisal is viewed as an isolated event, it is only natural that supervisors will come to view their responsibilities the same way, further propelling overall performance in a downward spiral. There should be no surprises at the appraisal.

- **Comparing employees:** If you want to create ill will among your staff, damage morale and destroy teamwork, just rank or compare your workers to one another. It's a guarantee of friction among them and hostility toward you.

- **Focusing on blame:** The goal of performance appraisal is to improve performance, not lay blame for failure. Managers who forget this end up developing staff members who don't trust or respect them. The appraisal process should be used to build the relationship between manager and employee … not to destroy it.

- **Believing a rating form is an objective, impartial tool:** All ratings are subjective!! All ratings are subject to appraiser bias (intentional or not).

- **Canceling or postponing appraisal meetings:** This gives the impression that the process is not very important … certainly not a priority. Managers should either commit to the process and give it priority status or skip it completely.

- **Measuring trivial things:** Sometimes the important things are hard to measure (e.g., overall quality of customer service), so managers fall prey to measuring inconsequential, quantifiable things (number of calls, how long phone rings before answering, tardiness, etc.). Not only does this not help the employee improve performance, but it shifts her focus to the unimportant … probably hurting performance in the long run.

- **Using the same procedures to assess all employees and all jobs:** One size does not fit all. A tool designed to review a supervisor is not appropriate to assess the receptionist. If the form appears adequate for both, it probably is truly appropriate and effective for neither.

Basic Skill-Building

First, you must be aware of your *attending behavior*. This refers to your general behavior while you are interacting with the employee. Let's look at the basic components of healthy behavior.

1. Make eye contact. Look the employee in the eye when talking AND listening.

2. Use good body language. Direct your body toward the listener; lean forward slightly. Use your facial muscles actively, but naturally. Don't be stone-faced and don't forget to smile occasionally!

3. Use gestures to support your facial message. Minimize distracting mannerisms, overused phrases or clichés. Don't reuse the same example and don't let distracting mannerisms get in your way so that the employee pays more attention to your mannerisms than your message. Practice your delivery in front of a mirror or videotape a mock interview. Study the videotape carefully in order to improve your communication ability.

4. Vary your speaking style to improve the chances that your message is heard and understood. When you are serious, make your points slowly and with emphasis. When you are enthusiastic, speed up and raise your pitch.

5. Become skilled at asking questions and gathering information. Invite your employee to talk. **Be prepared to stop talking and start listening at any time.** You are not on stage or carrying out a monologue here. This is not a lecture but a guided conversation.

6. As you become involved in discussion, focus attention on a specific topic, but give the employee latitude to respond. Get rid of the feeling of interrogation.

7. Watch for clues. Continuing to talk when you know a person is not listening is a waste of time. If the employee exhibits any of the following behaviors, it means she is not listening:

   • Holding out her hand as if to say "Stop"

   • Looking confused

   • Rolling her eyes toward the ceiling

- Beginning to interrupt

- Constantly looking away

What's the best way to avoid sounding like an interrogator? When questioning employees, the general rule is that it is better to be descriptive than judgmental, to be supportive rather than authoritarian, and to set a tone of equality, not superiority.

By being descriptive, not judgmental, you show the employee that you are interested in solving a problem, not in finding a scapegoat, someone to blame.

- *Judgmental:* "How could you do such a stupid thing?"

- *Descriptive:* "Can you explain what caused the problem?"

By being supportive, not authoritarian, you help eliminate resentfulness and defensiveness. It is better to show an attitude of respect for the employee's ability to solve problems.

- *Authoritarian:* "This is what you will do to solve this problem."

- *Supportive:* "What do you think we should do to solve this problem, and how can I help?"

If you put too much emphasis on your position and power, you may create a barrier between you and your employee. However, if you seek employee opinions and share information, a feeling of equality is created.

- *Superiority:* "I used to do your job, and this is the way it's done."

- *Equality:* "This is the way this has been done in the past, but I would like to hear how you think it could be done better."

Remember, you learn more from listening than from talking. The first highly effective listening technique is *reflecting,* or summarizing. This technique captures the gist of what the other person says, putting it in your words. It helps prevent misunderstanding and stimulates your thinking.

Reflecting an employee's feelings is a simple, two-part process:

1. You identify the feeling behind the other person's remark: confusion, anger, frustration, excitement, determination, etc.

2. You reflect the feeling back to the employee, beginning your response with words such as: "You're feeling … " or "Sounds as if you're feeling … ."

When you respond to, reflect or summarize an employee's feelings in this way, you send an important message: "I'm as interested in your feelings as I am in your thoughts and ideas."

Another fundamental communication technique is to speak in specific terms. Here are six ways to build effective communication skills during your appraisals:

1. Focus on the closing; speaking "fuzzily" is distracting and unproductive.

   • Fuzzy: "Work on your attitude."

   • Specific: "I need more work from you when my reports are due. OK?" Ask for more work.

2. Focus on the facts. Avoid emotionally loaded expressions or criticisms that include insulting words, e.g., "That was stupid."

3. Watch out for exaggeration, e.g., "That was the most ridiculous thing anyone could have said." Be specific and accurate in your comments.

How Not to Do It

"You have a bad temper. Stop throwing temper tantrums."

How to Do It

"You need to work on staying calm. Let's talk about some specific ways to do that."

---

4. Watch your pacing and timing. Pause after your main points, giving them a chance to sink in. Make sure the employee stays with you. Tell her what you're going to tell her, tell her, then tell her what you told her.

5. Strive for rapport. Reflecting feeling captures the emotions. Reflecting does not mean you agree with a statement. Using this technique, your task is only to mirror the employee's statement.

6. Summarize frequently. Summarizing focuses the main points.

Here are some points to remember:

- You do not make change happen by lecturing.

- We have little ability to get people to do things they do not want to do.

- The way people function is somehow part of them; they do not change easily.

- Resistance is softened when people feel they can discuss their opinions and be heard.

During the appraisal session, **you should do only 10 percent of the talking**. You are the catalyst of change, getting employees to do most of the talking. Most supervisors tend to dominate conversations. How do you change this?

- Learn to be quiet and understand the value of silence. Silence rarely offends. It is normally nonjudgmental if accompanied by the correct, open, attending behavior. The raised eyebrow with the expectant look, uncrossed arms and legs, and facing the employee directly are all examples of nonjudgmental silence that encourage your employee to talk.

- Know how to use questions effectively. You must become skilled in the use of the different types of questions. Be conscious of the kind of responses a question will generate before asking it. **It is the *form* of the question that determines the extent of the response.**

Restrictive or close-ended questions prevent thought-provoking answers and discourage productive discussion. Examples are: How long? When did you … ? Who wrote this?

Primarily, three types of questions work in getting employees to talk. Use these as alternatives to restrictive or closed questions:

- Open-ended Questions

- Reflective Questions

- Directive Questions

    1. Open-ended Questions

        Open-ended questions get at attitudes, feelings, opinions and other useful information about the person. Examples include: How do you feel about … ? What could we do to … ? Why has this … ?

        Open-ended questions can be successfully combined with the hypothetical problem. Examples include: Suppose you were … ? How would you do it if you were … ? What action would you take if … ?

Open-ended questions can also be combined with commands. For example: Tell me more … Give me more detail … Keep talking …

How to Do It

Employee: "Our results would improve if we modified the method we used to manufacture that part."

Supervisor: "You're convinced the results can be improved?"

---

2. Reflective Questions

Reflective questions can help you avoid arguments, because you are responding without accepting or rejecting what the employee says. It shows that you understand, that you are listening and that you hear what the employee is saying. This also implies that you understand how she feels. Reflective questions encourage employees to expand on what they have said, leading to deeper levels of communication and understanding. If an employee has said something illogical or untrue, hearing it repeated helps her see the problems in it.

How to Do It

"It sounds like something is really bothering you. Is there anything else you'd like to say?"

---

3. Directive Questions

Directive questions obtain specific information. Such questions are usually used after the other types of questions have been tried and communication between you and your employee is strong.

How to Do It

"If you're convinced the results can be improved, exactly what would you do and when would you do it?"

Combining different types of questions in your interview will stimulate the employee to participate. Pick the tools that are best for the job.

Once you get the employee talking, how do you respond to keep the conversation going? Use responses that focus and encourage, or the conversation will go off track or stop. Refrain from one-upmanship. Your objective is to stimulate the employee to suggest ideas. If you argue the merits of ideas as the employee says them, you waste idea-giving time. If you reject ideas as they are given, you may punish idea-giving behavior and discourage further discussion. If you reinforce good ideas when they come up before all ideas are out, it's easy for the employee to stop searching. A productive appraisal depends on the interaction of ideas. Some of the best ideas come from bad ideas, so stimulate the process and get *all* the ideas on the table.

How to Do It

Supervisor: Please tell me any problems you've been having.

Employee: The new computers are down more than they're up. Is somebody going to do something about that? I can't get my work done on time.

Supervisor: Sounds as if you're pretty angry about that.

Employee: I am!

Interviewing Attitudes

1. Avoid being defensive yourself — the person with tact gets things done without hostility.

2. Think positively about where you're trying to go rather than being negative about where you are now.

3. Think about growth, development, progress and accomplishment.

4. Don't use words that point to negative behavior. You are not trying to excuse the past; you're planning for a better future.

5. Don't use *never, ever, always, every time, invariably, without exception*, etc. These terms trigger negative responses. Avoid profanity. Your language should be tactful but firm.

6. Control the interview. Your control is essential to a productive interview and to getting the employee's commitment to plan an improvement.

7. Focus the interview so you and the employee have to work on solutions. Discuss possible ways to improve and decide how to begin.

8. Decide together what help the employee needs. Decide what you need to do to accomplish high-priority tasks. Be specific.

   - State the nature of the improvement sought.

   - State the quantity of the improvement sought.

   - Define dates when progress is to be checked.

   - Agree on who is going to do what.

Stay the course and communicate your message. Remember, the formal, sit-down performance appraisal interview is conversation that gets somewhere. It has objectives, an orderly track and results in concrete agreements. It is conversational, but the employee does most of the talking.

Another frequently overlooked but highly effective skill you should perfect is body language. Body language sometimes communicates more about a person's real feelings than the person can. The more skilled you become at watching body language and picking up on these signals, the more effective you will become during performance appraising. In the important and sensitive business of performance appraisals, it isn't an option, it's a necessity.

Equality can be expressed in everything, from the initial handshake to the image left at the close of the interview. It is important not to stand or tower over your employee during the performance appraisal, starting from the time you ask your employee to meet with you.

The next most important thing to watch is eye contact. Avoiding eye contact can indicate disagreement, an unwillingness to continue to talk or dishonesty. Confident people have more eye contact than those who are unsure or attempting to conceal, and the duration of their contact is longer. Confident people blink less, hence they also seem to be better listeners.

Gestures are almost as important as eye contact. One of the key gestures is crossing the arms across the chest as if to protect yourself against the individual, sometimes indicating you'd rather not move. Different from a comfortable position, this gesture usually involves gripping the arms or clenched fists.

Your response should be to draw out the feelings of subordinates who have crossed their arms and find out what their needs are. Reconsider what you are doing or saying to employees who have crossed their arms, because they are signalling strongly that they have withdrawn from the conversation. Getting agreement on anything, even on entirely unrelated topics, becomes more difficult after the arms are crossed and a person has become defensive. Failing to recognize the early signs of discontent or disagreement results in painful and unproductive communications.

Another key body language signal to watch out for is posture. Slouching can indicate indifference. Does the employee look interested? If not, find out why. A confident and open person will talk without covering her mouth and will stand and sit straight in an open posture.

In a study of negotiating techniques, it was found that the atmosphere for reaching settlements was enhanced when negotiators uncrossed their legs and moved toward each other.

Crossing of legs and leaning away are parts of a family of behaviors that communicate suspicion, uncertainty, rejection or doubt. Other examples of such behaviors include physically moving the body away from the person, having the feet or entire body pointing toward the exit, sending a sideways glance, taking a sideways position and squirming in the chair.

Watch your employee's body language for important clues. Even more important, evaluate your own body language so that it:

1. Sends positive messages about your openness, understanding and willingness to listen to the employee

2. Does not send messages of superiority, defensiveness or close-mindedness

1. Consider each of the common pitfalls below and assess which ones you find yourself succumbing to. If need be, refer to pages 93-95 to review each prior to completing this exercise.

	Often	Occasionally	Seldom	Never
Fear of failure				
The "fudge factor"				
Aversion to judging				
Positive feedback-seeking game				
Inadequate appraiser preparation				
Lack of employee participation				
Isolated, year-end reviews				
Comparing employees				
Focusing on blame				
Believing a rating form is an objective, impartial tool				
Canceling or postponing appraisal meetings				
Measuring trivial things				
Using the same procedures to assess all employees and all jobs				

2. After explaining each of the pitfalls above, ask your subordinates to complete the same exercise from their perspective. Be prepared for their perceptions to differ from yours.

3. Based on 1 and 2 above, outline a skill development plan for sharpening your performance appraisal skills. Specify the skills to be improved, the methods you will use to improve them and a timetable for implementation.

Reflections

9 FOLLOW-UP

Lack of follow-up is one of the most common supervisory failures. Improving your follow-up to performance appraisals is the essence of this chapter.

Informal follow-ups begin immediately after the appraisal interview. Follow-up immediately and touch base frequently. Remember, the appraisal process is a day-in, day-out, never-ending, year-round feedback loop.

Both formal and informal follow-up are critical to improving performance and strengthening your relationship with your employee. Ask your employee to follow up with you. Be sure he knows you meant what you said about working together by staying on top of what you agreed to work on together. Answer any questions immediately. These actions solidify the two-way relationship between you and your employee and make certain that the spotlight isn't totally on the employee.

> **Feedback is not about forms.**
>
> **Feedback delayed is feedback denied.**
>
> **Giving people a raise is not the same as giving them feedback.**
>
> **Always get feedback on your feedback.**

Reinforce changed behavior immediately! Reward effort. It is better to praise positive behavior than to criticize negative behavior. Do this as behavior occurs; don't wait for the next formal meeting. Changing behavior is hard work. In many instances, achieving the desired behavior may require a number of intermediate behavior modifications. Recognize steps in the right direction — no matter how small those steps may be. Periodic encouragement from you is necessary to prevent the employee from returning to the inappropriate behavior. The most critical aspect of follow-up is timeliness.

The structure of the follow-up interview is similar to that of the original performance appraisal interview. Analyze both your employee's and your own performance. Review progress; ask the employee's opinion and give your own. Verify agreement on all main points before proceeding to the negative issues.

Decide where you want to go. For example, if major progress has been made, you can afford to schedule the next formal follow-up meeting further into the future. If little progress has been made but a lot of effort has been expended, you can renegotiate the agreement, adjusting the "when" aspect. You may revise your goals, taking smaller steps. If, on the other hand, little progress has been made and little effort has been expended, this may signal that a termination is in order. Ask the employee for solutions. Ask the employee to think about the consequences of nonperformance, i.e., demotion, termination, etc.

Your next step is to close the interview. Get the employee's overall reaction to how things went. Give your own thoughts and feelings as well. Schedule your next follow-up meeting to make sure you and your employee accomplish your goals! End the interview on a positive note.

Performance appraisals are most effective when done
on an ongoing basis — not once a year!

Use this list to evaluate where you are with each employee and what type of feedback/follow-up process to put into place. Each time a follow-up meeting takes place, review each of these elements to ensure success.

- Where do we stand?

- What are specific areas of improvement/success?

- Have the goals been accomplished?

- In what specific ways have the goals been exceeded or missed?

- If a goal was not achieved, was progress made?

- What obstacles stand in the way of success?

- What can be done to overcome those obstacles?

- What can you do to help?

- What is the new targeted timetable for achievement?

- What are the consequences of failure?

- When will the next formal follow-up session occur?

Reflections

10 FORMS, PRACTICES AND CHECKLISTS

Performance Appraisal Checklist

Preparation

_____ I have reviewed mutually understood expectations with respect to job duties, projects, goals, standards and any performance factors pertinent to this appraisal discussion.

_____ I have measured job performance against mutually understood expectations. I have done my best to avoid such pitfalls as:

- Allowing bias/prejudice to be a factor

- Not consulting my performance log and relying on my memory alone

- Overly focusing on some aspects of the job at the expense of others

- Being overly influenced by my own experience

- Using trait evaluation rather than performance measurement

_____ I have reviewed the employee's background, including:

- Skills

- Work experience

- Training

- Past performance

- Attendance records

_____ I have identified the employee's performance strengths and determined areas in need of improvement. In so doing, I have:

- Accumulated specific documentation to communicate my position

- Limited myself to those critical points that are the most important

- Prepared a development plan in case the employee needs assistance in coming up with a suitable plan

- Identified areas for concentration for the next appraisal period

- Given the employee advance notice of when the discussion will be held so that she can prepare

- Set aside an adequate block of uninterrupted time to permit a full and complete discussion

Conducting the Appraisal Discussion

_____ I plan to begin the discussion by creating a sincere, open and friendly atmosphere. This includes:

- Reviewing the purpose of the discussion

- Making it clear that it is a joint discussion for the purpose of mutual problem-solving and goal-setting

- Striving to put the employee at ease

_____ In the body of the discussion, I intend to keep the focus on job performance and related factors. These include:

- Discussing job requirements, employee strengths, accomplishments and improvements needed; evaluating results of performance against objectives set during previous reviews and discussions

- Being prepared to cite observations for each point I want to discuss

- Encouraging the employee to appraise her own performance

- Using open-ended, reflective and directive questions to promote thought

_____ I will encourage the employee to outline her personal plans for self-development before suggesting ideas of my own. In the process, I will:

- Get the employee to set growth and improvement targets.

- Reach agreement on appropriate development plans, set a timetable and explain the support I am prepared to give.

- Be prepared to discuss work assignments, projects and goals for the next appraisal period, asking the employee to prepare suggestions.

Closing the Discussion

_____ I will be prepared to make notes during the discussion for the purpose of summarizing agreements and follow-up. In closing, I will:

- Summarize what has been discussed.

- Show enthusiasm for plans that have been made.

- Give the employee an opportunity to make additional suggestions.

- End on a positive, friendly, harmonious note.

Post-Appraisal Follow-Up

_____   As soon as the discussion is over, I will record the plans made, points requiring follow-up and the commitments I made. I will provide a copy for the employee. I will also evaluate:

- How I handled the discussion

- What I did well

- What I could have done better

- What I learned about the employee and her job

- What I learned about myself and my job

Reviewing the Performance Appraisal System

Place a circle around the number indicating the importance of your performance appraisal system in achieving the goals listed below. Then, have your employees do the same and compare their responses with yours.

Scale: 5 — Always   4 — Usually   3 — Occasionally   2 — Seldom   1 — Never

Goals		Yours	Employees
1. Increase employees' understanding of job role and employer's expectations	5 4 3 2 1	_____	_____
2. Improve employee morale	5 4 3 2 1	_____	_____
3. Uphold professional standards	5 4 3 2 1	_____	_____
4. Increase employees' self-awareness of job performance	5 4 3 2 1	_____	_____
5. Maintain discipline	5 4 3 2 1	_____	_____
6. Reward superior performance	5 4 3 2 1	_____	_____
7. Produce competition among employees	5 4 3 2 1	_____	_____
8. Reinforce boss-employee relationship	5 4 3 2 1	_____	_____
9. Improve employee performance skills	5 4 3 2 1	_____	_____
10. Weed out inferior employees	5 4 3 2 1	_____	_____
11. Increase employees' self-confidence and self-esteem	5 4 3 2 1	_____	_____
12. Inform supervisors/upper management of employees' performance	5 4 3 2 1	_____	_____
13. Provide basis for awards and/or promotions	5 4 3 2 1	_____	_____
14. Improve supervisor-employee relationship	5 4 3 2 1	_____	_____
15. Provide basis for changing financial compensation	5 4 3 2 1	_____	_____
16. Other: _____	5 4 3 2 1	_____	_____

KEY STRATEGY: Both supervisor and employee must complete this review.

Performance Evaluation

1. Valid
   - Has a job analysis been conducted recently to determine the duties and responsibilities that must be carried out if the job is to be done successfully?
   - Are performance standards based on the results of the job analysis?

2. Consistent
   - Is the system implemented consistently (does a procedure exist)?
   - Is the same system used for all employees?
   - Do people who do the same work get evaluated against the same standards?
   - Are managers trained to use the system?

3. Useful
   - Is the system perceived to be helpful?
   - Is there support from top management?
   - Is the system easy to administer?

Key Point

The use of any decision-making procedure (i.e., test for selection; applications; resumes; performance appraisal forms for use in promotion, demotion, transfer, discipline, termination and salary actions) that has an adverse impact on any protected group is considered discriminatory — UNLESS that decision-making procedure accurately measures the qualifications required for success in the job.

❑ We're OK   ❑ Review   ❑ Action needed

❑ Person responsible _____

Documentation Checklist

Directions: Use this checklist to ensure that you have included all important components of relevant documentation.

Date _____   Employee _____

Actions   **Date(s)**

❑   1. Copies of previous performance appraisal   _____

❑   2. Documented evidence of performance problem   _____

❑   3. Verbal warning   _____

❑   4. Written warning   _____

❑   5. Personal interview(s)   _____

❑   6. Remedial actions: _____

      • Type _____   _____

      • Attempted _____   _____

      • Documented _____   _____

❑   7. Consequences interview   _____

❑   8. Check with personnel department   _____

❑   9. Check with next upper-management level   _____

❑   10. Check with legal department or other legal resource   _____

❑   11. Termination notification   _____

❑   12. Termination interview   _____

❑   13. Explain rights   _____

❑   14. Exit interview   _____

❑   15. Debriefing with staff   _____

Contracting With the Employee: A Corrective Action Plan

Employee name _____

_____   _____
Date   Job title

_____   _____
Time   Meeting place

Specific problem to be addressed:

Strategy:

Action steps (expectations):

Timetable:

Handling Problem Employees

Establish Misconduct Policy

Examples:

1. Theft over $10
2. Sexual harassment
3. Major insubordination
4. Obscene/abusive language
5. Asleep on the job
6. Leaving job without permission

ORAL NOTICE
Tell 'em...

WRITTEN NOTICE
Tell 'em what you told 'em...

SUSPENSION
(Final written notice)

TERMINATION

- Discipline is at management's discretion based on an employee's position, employment record and mitigating circumstances.

- Similar instances of misconduct will be handled on an individual basis.

Tips for Discipline

- Fairness
- Open-mindedness
- Timeliness
- Consistency
- Objectivity
- Documentation
- Communication
- Progression

❏ We're OK   ❏ Review   ❏ Action needed

❏ Person responsible _____

119

How to Get the Employee to Talk

1. Inform the employee, "This position is important to our company, and we feel we must make the best possible decision."

2. Ask the employee, "Does that make sense to you? Do you agree? What do you think we should do?" to see if she understands.

3. Continue with the employee, "The more information we have, the better decisions we can make for our company and for you. Do you agree?" to see if she still understands.

4. Say to the employee, "I feel it is important to talk directly with your peers. Do you have any problems with that?" (Watch closely for the reaction.)

5. Ask the employee, "When I talk with your co-workers, what will they tell me about ... ?" (Start with easy questions.)

6. State as a final comment, "I don't like surprises! Is there anything you would like to explain now before I talk with your former supervisors?"

Written Warnings — A Short Course

Before documenting unacceptable performance or behavior, be sure you understand the entire situation. Be sure you can answer the following:

WHO?   Who was involved? Who reported the incident? Who witnessed the incident? Who was affected?

WHAT?   What specifically happened? What were the results of the action or inaction?

WHERE?   Where did the incident occur?

WHY?   Why did this incident happen — what procedures or rules weren't followed? What is the employee's reason for the incident or behavior?

WHEN?   When did the incident occur? When was it reported? When was the employee given the proper procedures or rules? When was the employee given any other notices of unacceptable performance?

HOW?   How did this incident happen? What did the employee do or fail to do? How did it affect others or the association? How could the incident have been avoided?

There are some simple rules regarding written warnings. After you have investigated the incident or behavior, use the following as a checklist in preparing your document.

- Prepare a neat and readable written warning.

- Address the warning to the employee, date it and sign it.

- Always give the specific details — who, what, where, why, when, how — of the incident or behavior.

- Avoid subjective statements; emphasize association policies and procedures.

- Offer solutions and state objectives.

- Document the consequences of continued unacceptable behavior, e.g., " ... failure to ... will result in further disciplinary action up to and including termination."

Conducting a Firing Interview

1. Do your homework.

2. If the situation seems to call for it, have a "friendly witness" present during the session.

3. Give clear, specific reasons for the termination. Put these in writing, signed by both parties.

4. Help the employee realize that once the consequences were explained to her, continuation of the unsatisfactory behavior was the employee's matter.

5. Focus the termination on unacceptable behavior, not on the person.

6. If it is applicable, advise the employee of the implications of removing files, equipment or other organizational property, as well as revealing trade secrets to competitors.

7. Not all employees will take termination calmly, although the termination should come as no surprise. If the employee becomes upset, these steps will help:

   a. Listen

   b. Share

   c. Continue

   d. Above all, stay in control of your own emotions. There's no need for you to feel threatened by words.

   e. If you are physically threatened, and there is no one with you, call in someone else immediately.

8. Know company policies.

9. Let employees know where they stand with you. Will you provide references? A final word: Your anxiety about the termination session is both normal and healthy — it is a sign that you are a caring, feeling person, involved with a difficult task.

10. Help employees realize that termination is painful for everyone; you and the organization would like everyone to succeed — and you wish them well.

❏ We're OK   ❏ Review   ❏ Action needed

❏ Person responsible _____

INDEX

U

W

NOTES

Buy any 3, get 1 FREE!

Get a 60-Minute Training Series™ Handbook FREE ($14.95 value)*
when you buy any three. See back of order form for full selection of titles.

These are helpful how-to books for you, your employees and co-workers. Add to
your library. Use for new-employee training, brown-bag seminars, promotion gifts and
more. Choose from many popular titles on a variety of lifestyle, communication, productivity
and leadership topics. Exclusively from National Press Publications.

BUY 3 GET 1 FREE! Buy more, save more!

DESKTOP HANDBOOK ORDER FORM

Ordering is easy:

1. Complete both sides of this Order Form, detach, and mail, fax or phone your order to:

   Mail: National Press Publications
   P.O. Box 41907
   Kansas City, MO 64141-6107

   Fax: 1-913-432-0824
   Phone: 1-800-258-7248 (in Canada 1-800-685-4142)
   Internet: http://www.natsem.com/books.html

2. Please print:

   Name_____ Position/Title _____

   Company/Organization_____

   Address_____City _____

   State/Province_____ZIP/Postal Code _____

   Telephone (____)_____ Fax (____) _____

3. Easy payment:

   ❑ Enclosed is my check or money order for $_____ (total from back).
   Please make payable to National Press Publications.

   Please charge to:
   ❑ MasterCard   ❑ VISA   ❑ American Express

   Credit Card No. _____ Exp. Date_____

   Signature_____

   •

   ### MORE WAYS TO SAVE:

   SAVE 33%!!! BUY 20-50 COPIES of any title ... pay just $9.95 each ($11.25 Canadian).

   SAVE 40%!!! BUY 51 COPIES OR MORE of any title ... pay just $8.95 each ($10.25 Canadian).

   * $16.25 in Canada

Buy 3, get 1 FREE!
60-MINUTE TRAINING SERIES™ HANDBOOKS

TITLE	RETAIL PRICE	QTY	TOTAL
8 Steps for Highly Effective Negotiations #424	$14.95		
Assertiveness #4422	$14.95		
Balancing Career and Family #415	$14.95		
Delegate for Results #4592	$14.95		
Dynamic Communication Skills for Women #413	$14.95		
Exceptional Customer Service #4882	$14.95		
Fear & Anger: Slay the Dragons… #4302	$14.95		
Getting Things Done #4112	$14.95		
How to Coach an Effective Team #4308	$14.95		
How to De-Junk Your Life #4306	$14.95		
How to Handle Conflict and Confrontation #4952	$14.95		
How to Manage Your Boss #493	$14.95		
How to Supervise People #4102	$14.95		
How to Work with People #4032	$14.95		
Inspire & Motivate Through Performance Reviews #4232	$14.95		
Listen Up: Hear What's Really Being Said #4172	$14.95		
Motivation and Goal-Setting #4962	$14.95		
A New Attitude #4432	$14.95		
Parenting: Ward & June… #486	$14.95		
The Polished Professional #426	$14.95		
The Power of Innovative Thinking #428	$14.95		
The Power of Self-Managed Teams #4222	$14.95		
Powerful Communication Skills #4132	$14.95		
Powerful Leadership Skills for Women #463	$14.95		
Present with Confidence #4612	$14.95		
The Secret to Developing Peak Performers #4692	$14.95		
Self-Esteem: The Power to Be Your Best #4642	$14.95		
Shortcuts to Organized Files & Records #4307	$14.95		
The Stress Management Handbook #4842	$14.95		
Supreme Teams: How to Make Teams Work #4303	$14.95		
Techniques to Improve Your Writing Skills #460	$14.95		
Thriving on Change #4212	$14.95		
The Write Stuff #414	$14.95		

Sales Tax		
Sales Tax	**Subtotal**	$
All purchases subject to state and local sales tax. Questions? Call **1-800-258-7248**	**Add 7% Sales Tax** (*Or add appropriate state and local tax*)	$
	Shipping and Handling (*$3 one item; 50¢ each additional item*)	$
	TOTAL	$